RAISING BACKYARD CHICKENS

30-DAY GUIDE TO RAISING HAPPY CHICKENS FOR
EGGS AND MEAT, PROVIDING COMPLETE
INFORMATION ON BREEDS, HOUSING, FEEDING,
HEALTH CARE AND MORE!

TYLER BRISTOL

LEANN BRISTOL

PUBLISHING

CONTENTS

Unlock the secrets to successful chicken raising with our exclusive bonus content, available nowhere else! Scan the QR code to access your free bonus content and make your chicken-keeping journey a breeze.

Scan the QR code to access your free resources and sign up to get new ebook releases sent straight to your inbox!

INTRODUCTION

"There are days when I am envious of my hens, when I hunger for a purpose as perfect and sure as a single daily egg."

— BARBARA KINGSOLVER, U.S. AUTHOR

Keeping and rearing chickens is a time-honored tradition that has been practiced by people all over the world for centuries. You are not alone if you dream of keeping a flock of backyard hens. In 2018, the American Pet Producers Survey found that more than 10 million U.S. households were raising chickens!

There are numerous advantages to rearing chickens, and most people dream of a constant supply of fresh, organic eggs from happy, fluffy hens. Raising chickens can be essential to sustainable living, providing a source of eggs and meat for families while reducing reliance on industrial agriculture and the food supply chain. It can also be a valuable educational experience for children, teaching them about responsibility, compassion, and the natural world.

However, caring for a flock of living, breathing birds can be daunting for new chicken keepers. It can take time to figure out where to start. You will undoubtedly have many unanswered questions – how many chickens do you need, what sort of hens are best for your needs, and how do you feed them and keep them safe and healthy?

Raising backyard chickens has become a popular activity for people of all ages and backgrounds. Whether you're interested in providing fresh, healthy eggs for your family, enjoying the companionship of feathered friends, or simply connecting with nature, keeping chickens can be a rewarding and enjoyable experience.

Setting up a backyard chicken flock can also help provide you and your family with food security. There is no better feeling than collecting a clutch of fresh eggs every day, and your chickens can also provide a regular source of organic meat. Chickens quickly become part of the natural cycle of your home life, eating your waste food and reducing pests around the yard while also providing eggs for you to enjoy.

This book is designed to be a comprehensive guide for beginners just starting out with backyard chickens, but it contains detailed information essential to chicken keepers of all experience levels. You will find practical advice and tips based on years of experience from seasoned chicken keepers, a 30-day timeline to streamline the process, as well as helpful resources to guide you through each step of the journey. It covers everything you need to know about all aspects of chicken care, ranging from a proper coop set up to protecting your birds from predators and disease. By the end of this book, readers will have all the knowledge and confidence they need to successfully raise happy and healthy chickens in their own backyard.

There are also detailed sections on the legalities of keeping chickens in your backyard and factors to consider before setting up your new chicken enterprise. Including choosing the right type, breed, and number of chickens to ensure your flock is happy, healthy, and productive. Chicken breeds are hugely diverse in appearance, attributes, and care needs, and it is important to understand this as some of the more exotic, high-maintenance breeds may only lay one or two eggs a week!

The book emphasizes the importance of humane and ethical treatment of your birds. Raising chickens is a responsibility that should be taken seriously, and it is our duty as stewards of these animals to give them the best possible care. This means providing them with a comfortable and safe living environment, feeding them a nutritious and balanced diet, and treating them with kindness and respect.

Along the way, readers will learn some great tips and tricks to help keep their flock in good health, such as how to grow food for them and easy ways to provide environmental enrichment. If readers are worried about the antibiotics and hormones used in commercial farming, raising their own backyard hens is a wallet-friendly and satisfying way to enjoy organic meat for their families.

Ultimately, this book is about more than just raising chickens. It's about connecting with nature, living sustainably, and building a better world for ourselves and our communities. By learning about chicken husbandry, readers can rediscover the joys of simple living and create a more humane and sustainable world for all.

Whether you're a backyard hobbyist, a small-scale farmer, or simply interested in sustainable living, we invite you to join us on this journey of discovery and learning.

"By diving into the world of raising backyard chickens, you're not just getting delicious eggs and meat for your family, but also immersing yourself in a timeless tradition that's been passed down for generations. Let's embark on this exciting journey of chicken husbandry together, exploring all the wonders and rewards it has to offer. We hope you enjoy every step of the way, just as much as we enjoyed writing this book!"

— TYLER & LEANN BRISTOL

YOUR 30-DAY BACKYARD CHICKEN ADVENTURE TIMELINE

This is a suggested 30-day timeline, which can vary depending on your situation. We hope you feel more confident after reading our book and are ready to get started!

Week 1: Research and Preparation

Day 1-2: Knowledge is Power

Welcome to your backyard chicken journey! Begin by diving into research about raising chickens. Learn about chicken breeds, their specific needs, and common challenges. The resources included with this book are a great place to start! There are QR codes at the end of the chapters that are linked to these resources.

Day 3-4: Climate and Breed Selection

Consider your local climate and choose chicken breeds that are well-suited to thrive in your area. Look for breeds known for their adaptability, cold or heat tolerance, and depending on your goals, their egg-laying capacity or meat production. Find resources online or connect with fellow chicken keepers to gather valuable insights.

Day 5-7: Legalities and Local Regulations

Investigate local laws and regulations regarding backyard chicken keeping. Check your municipality's website or reach out to local authorities for guidance. Additionally, connect with other chicken keepers in your area, possibly through social media groups, to get advice on navigating the legal aspects.

Week 2: Housing and Setup

Day 8-12: Coop Construction

Based on your research and legal requirements, start building your chicken coop. Ensure it is secure, well-ventilated, and provides adequate space for your future flock. Please seek advice from other local chicken keepers who can share their experiences and tips on an efficient coop setup. Depending on your climate, Your needs might differ from what you see online, so local advice is extremely valuable. Most of the time, your fellow chicken keepers will happily help answer questions to get you started.

Day 13-16: Run Design and Safety

As you construct the coop, plan and set up your chicken run. Focus on creating a predator-proof environment with sturdy fencing or hardware cloth. Explore online resources such as social media groups and online forums dedicated to backyard chicken keeping to gather insights on run design, safety measures, and enrichment ideas. Runs are not one-size-fits-all, but you may find plans you can follow and make adjustments to that will be perfect for your space.

Week 3: Essential Supplies and Preparations

Day 17-19: Feeders and Waterers

Purchase durable and appropriate feeders and waterers for your chickens. Ensure they are suitable to your needs, and large enough to accommodate your growing flock. Choose quality chicken feed suitable for their age and consider adding supplements if needed.

Day 20-22: Health and Safety

Research common chicken health issues and preventive measures. Find a local veterinarian and establish a relationship for check-ups or emergencies. Purchase essential health supplies like a first aid kit, supplements, and parasite treatments.

Week 4: Welcoming Your Feathered Friends

Day 23-26: Ordering Chicks, Hens, Pullets, or Eggs

Based on your breed selection, connect with reputable hatcheries or local breeders to order chicks, hens, roosters, pullets, or acquire fertilized eggs. Coordinate the delivery or pickup dates. If you're getting eggs or chicks, prepare a brooder box with proper bedding, heat source, and feed.

Day 27-30: Brooding and Care

Set up the brooder box, ensuring a warm and safe environment for your chicks. Monitor their temperature, provide clean water, and introduce them to their first feed. Observe and care for them diligently during this critical stage of their development.

Authors' Note: Research and preparation are vital for a successful backyard chicken experience. Seek knowledge from various sources, including fellow chicken keepers in your area. Join social media groups or online forums to connect with like-minded individuals who can offer advice and guidance specific to your location. Have fun and enjoy the rewarding experience of raising your own chickens!

Scan the QR code to access your free resources

CHICKEN PLANET

*D*id you know that chickens are the closest living relative to the Tyrannosaurus rex? Chickens are descended from theropod dinosaurs, the same group of dinosaurs that this magnificent creature belonged to. Imagine a bunch of tiny dinosaurs roaming around your backyard – what fun!

However, before you rush out to buy your own little flock of dinosaur descendants, there are several legal and practical considerations to think about.

So, to start with, let's dive into everything you need to consider before raising your own chickens.

PART 1: THE LEGALITIES OF RAISING BACKYARD CHICKENS

The single most important thing to determine is whether or not rearing chickens is legal in your area. This is crucial because laws and regulations vary by location, and not following them could result in fines, penalties, or even legal action.

WHY DO LOCAL LAWS FOR RAISING BACKYARD CHICKENS MATTER?

Local laws for raising backyard chickens govern whether or not it is legal to keep chickens on your property and what specific rules and regulations must be followed. These laws are designed to protect not only the chickens' health, safety, and well-being but the surrounding community.

For example, local laws may dictate how many chickens can be kept on a property, how far they must be kept from neighboring properties, and what types of enclosures or fencing are required. They may also address noise, odor, and waste disposal stipulations.

By following these laws, backyard chicken keepers can help ensure that their chickens are healthy and well-cared for and that they are not causing any harm or nuisance to their neighbors or the community. Failure to comply with these laws can result in fines, penalties, or even legal action.

In addition to the legal implications, understanding and following local laws can also help foster positive relationships with neighbors and increase the overall acceptance of backyard chicken keeping in your community. It's crucial to do your research and be aware of the specific laws and regulations in your area before embarking on a backyard chicken-keeping venture. The last thing you want is a legal battle with the city or even your Homeowners Association if you are a part of one.. Don't worry; it shouldn't be too hard.

LAWS FOR RAISING CHICKENS IN VARIOUS STATES

Laws and regulations related to raising chickens can vary widely by state and even by individual cities or towns within a state. Some states have relatively lenient laws that allow for keeping backyard chickens with few restrictions, while others have more stringent requirements or outright bans on backyard poultry.

Here are some examples of the laws for raising chickens in various states and municipalities as they stand at the time of writing:

- In Los Angeles, California, residents can keep up to five hens for personal use in most residential areas as long as they meet certain zoning requirements and obtain a permit from the city.

- Residents in Seattle, Washington, are permitted to keep up to eight chickens per household as long as they comply with zoning and noise regulations.

- In Chicago, Illinois, households can keep up to six chickens on their property as long as they obtain a permit and meet certain requirements related to coop size, placement, and sanitation.

- Residents in New York City, New York allowed to keep up to six hens on their property as long as they comply with zoning regulations and obtain a permit from the city.

- In Portland, Oregon, residents can keep up to three

hens without a permit, as long as they comply with zoning and sanitation regulations.

It's important to note that these laws and regulations are subject to change, and backyard chicken keepers should always do their due diligence to research the most up-to-date laws in their specific location.

HOW TO FIND AND UNDERSTAND YOUR LOCAL LAWS REGARDING RAISING CHICKENS

If you're interested in raising chickens in your backyard, the best place to start is by researching the local laws and regulations related to chicken keeping in your area. The following steps will help you find the information you need:

- Check your city or county's website: Many municipalities have information about local laws and regulations related to backyard chicken keeping on their website. Look for sections on zoning, animal control, or health and safety.

- Contact your local government offices: If you need help finding the information online, reach out to your city or county government offices, such as the zoning department or animal control. They can provide you with information on any laws and regulations that may apply to backyard chicken keeping in your area.

- Consult with a local veterinarian: A local veterinarian with some expertise in chicken care can most likely provide insight into any local laws or regulations related to chicken keeping in your area.

- If you are in a Homeowners Association, check their website or call to ask if keeping chickens is alright. Better safe than sorry.

- Talk to other backyard chicken keepers in your area: If there are other backyard chicken keepers in your area, they may be able to provide insight into any local laws or regulations they have had to follow.

Once you have found information on your local laws and regulations related to backyard chicken keeping, take the time to carefully review and understand the requirements. Pay attention to any restrictions on the number of chickens, coop design and location, and waste disposal requirements. By understanding and following these laws, you can help ensure that your backyard chicken-keeping venture is both legal and successful.

HOW TO AVOID NUISANCE COMPLAINTS

Raising chickens in your backyard can be a rewarding and enjoyable experience, but it is essential to be mindful of your neighbors and take steps to avoid nuisance complaints. Here are some tips to help you keep your neighbors on board with your backyard chicken-keeping project:

- Be respectful of your neighbors: Talk to your neighbors about your plans to raise chickens, and address any concerns they may have. Keep your chickens and their coop clean and well-maintained to avoid unpleasant odors or pests.

- Keep noise levels low: Roosters can be noisy and disruptive, so consider only keeping hens, or ensure that your roosters are kept in a soundproofed coop or well away from your neighbors.

- Keep your chickens contained: Chickens are notorious for roaming and getting into places they shouldn't be, and they can be very destructive in the process. Ensure that your chickens are properly contained within a secure coop or run to prevent them from wandering onto neighboring properties.

- Dispose of waste properly: Chicken manure can be a valuable fertilizer, but it can also be smelly and attract pests. Ensure that chicken coops are cleaned regularly to minimize flies. Properly dispose of chicken waste in a compost bin or use it as a soil amendment in your garden, away from your neighbor's property.

- Follow local laws and regulations: Understanding and following local laws and regulations related to backyard chicken keeping can help you avoid nuisance complaints and legal trouble.

By being a responsible backyard chicken keeper and following these tips, you can help ensure that your neighbors are happy and that your backyard chicken-keeping experience is a positive one. Fostering these relationships is also vital if you plan on selling eggs, as it is highly likely that your friends, family, and neighbors will be your first customers!

THE HISTORY OF LOCAL LAWS FOR RAISING BACKYARD CHICKENS

Does it seem odd to you that there are so many stringent laws around chicken keeping? Well, when you delve into the history behind this legislation, you can start to understand why.

The history of local laws related to backyard chicken keeping in the United States is complex and varied. In the early 20th century, many urban areas had laws prohibiting backyard chicken keeping due to concerns about noise, odors, and disease. However, during World War I and II, government agencies encouraged urban residents to keep chickens as a way to supplement food supplies and support the war effort. As a result, many cities and towns relaxed their laws around backyard chicken keeping.

During the 1960s and 1970s, the urban homesteading movement sparked a renewed enthusiasm for backyard chicken keeping. As a result, numerous cities and towns reconsidered their regulations and started allowing chickens to be kept in residential areas again. However, the backyard chicken trend also led to complaints about noise, odors, and other issues, and many municipalities responded by enacting more restrictive laws and regulations around backyard chicken keeping.

Today, many cities and towns have laws and regulations that allow for backyard chicken keeping with certain restrictions, such as limitations on the number of chickens, requirements for coop size and design, and prohibitions on roosters. Some areas may have more stringent requirements, while others may prohibit backyard chicken keeping altogether.

As backyard chicken keeping continues to grow in popularity, local laws and regulations will likely continue to evolve and adapt to meet the needs and concerns of both backyard chicken keepers and their neighbors.

WHAT CAN YOU DO IF CHICKENS ARE NOT PERMITTED IN YOUR NEIGHBORHOOD?

If chickens are not permitted in your neighborhood, don't give up on your chicken-rearing dreams! There are a few other options you could consider to get around these poultry-keeping bans.

In some areas, you can apply for a zoning variance or a special-use permit to keep chickens on your property, even if they are not typically allowed. With the support of your neighbors and other potential chicken owners, you could also petition your local authority to see if a relaxation in the laws is feasible.

If you are interested in raising chickens for eggs or meat, you may be able to join a community garden or urban farm that allows you to keep chickens on their property. This can be a great way to get involved in a local food community and learn more about sustainable agriculture.

Another alternative is to find a nearby farm or agricultural property that allows you to keep chickens. Some farms may even offer programs where you can adopt chickens and receive eggs or meat in exchange for helping to care for the birds.

PART 2: CALCULATING HOW MANY CHICKENS YOU CAN REAR

Once you've confirmed that chicken rearing is permitted in your neighborhood, the next thing to figure out is how many chickens you can keep on your property.

This number can depend on a variety of factors, including the size of your property and your local zoning laws. You will also need to consider the amount of time space and resources you have available to care for your birds, and the potential for noise and odor.

Whether you're a beginner chicken farmer or an experienced homesteader, understanding how to calculate your flock size is essential for creating a safe and healthy environment for your birds and ensuring that you comply with local regulations.

WHAT IS THE MAXIMUM PERMITTED NUMBER OF BACKYARD CHICKENS?

The maximum permitted number of backyard chickens varies depending on the local laws and regulations of your area. Some municipalities have no restrictions on the number of chickens that can be kept, while others may have strict limits.

It is important to note that many municipalities require that you apply for a permit to keep chickens, and you also need to meet certain requirements related to coop size, placement, and sanitation.

Generally, the maximum permitted number of chickens is often determined by factors such as the property size, the proximity of neighboring homes, and the capacity of the coop and run. For example, a small urban lot may have a limit of four or six chickens, while a larger rural property may be able to accommodate more.

We've emphasized it before, but it cannot be stressed enough: thoroughly research the local laws and regulations concerning backyard chicken keeping in your area. It is crucial to determine the maximum number of chickens allowed. Failure to comply with these laws can lead to fines, legal issues, and even the unfortunate loss of your beloved chickens.

However, it is not just the legalities you need to think about – attempting to keep too many chickens in a small backyard can lead to sick, unhealthy, and unproductive birds. Just because the law says you can have four, six, or eight hens, doesn't mean you should necessarily do so!

DO YOU HAVE ENOUGH SPACE TO REAR BACKYARD CHICKENS?

Chickens need adequate space to live healthy and happy lives. The amount of space required depends on several factors, including the breed, and the purpose for which the chicken is being kept.

In general, a good rule of thumb is to provide at least 2-3 square feet of indoor space per chicken in the coop and at least 8-10 square feet of outdoor space per chicken in the run. For example, if you have four chickens, you should provide a coop with at least 8-12 square feet and a run with at least 32-40 square feet.

Additionally, the coop should be tall enough to allow the birds to stand up straight and move around comfortably. It should also have proper ventilation, nesting boxes, and roosting bars. For your own comfort and convenience, it is helpful to build a coop tall enough for you to stand up in.

It's important to note that these are minimum space requirements, and providing more space is always better. Chickens that are crowded or confined to small spaces can become stressed and agitated and may exhibit negative behaviors such as feather-pecking or even cannibalism. Providing plenty of space and enrichment in the form of perches, roosts, and nesting boxes can help keep chickens happy and healthy.

Additionally, some breeds of chickens may require more or less space depending on their size and activity levels. It's important to research the specific breed or breeds of chickens you plan to keep to ensure that you are providing adequate space and resources for their needs.

PART 3: FACTORS TO CONSIDER BEFORE RAISING CHICKENS

Okay, so you can legally keep chickens and you have the space; what's to stop you from rushing out to purchase your first hens? The dream of collecting eggs every day from your flock of feathered friends may seem very tempting, but it pays to consider the realities of owning chickens first!

Here are some of the aspects of chicken raising that first-timers should be aware of:

Egg production is not always consistent.

If you expect your new hens to start laying straight away, you might be disappointed! Young hens are often advertised as 'point of lay,' meaning they are just about old enough to start laying eggs. However, there can be a gap of several weeks or months between bringing the chickens home and when they start to lay. It is also important to note that some hens don't lay eggs year-round. Their egg production can be affected by several factors, including age, breed, and environmental conditions. Be prepared for periods where you feed and nurture your hens with very little return.

Chickens can live to be 10 to 12 years old, so raising them is a long-term commitment! Older hens tend to lay fewer eggs, so an aging flock can be expensive to feed and give you very few eggs. It is not always possible to figure out which hens are no longer laying, so culling them may not be an option.

Chickens can be destructive.

If you've never kept chickens before, you'll be amazed at how destructive they can be. They will quickly turn their run into a bare patch of ground, which can become a muddy mess in the winter. Many people dream of keeping free-range chickens, but the practicalities of this are not always feasible. They may scratch up your lawn or garden and wreak havoc in a vegetable plot. If your chickens were to escape into a neighbor's yard, they could quickly cause a large amount of damage.

Roosters are noisy. There is a good reason why many local authorities do not permit roosters in urban areas – male chickens are notoriously loud! They have no respect for human sleep patterns and will start crowing long before dawn. Many roosters crow every hour like clockwork! It is important to note that you don't need a rooster to get eggs. Hens will lay eggs regardless of whether or not there is a rooster present. But, if you want to rear chicks, you will either need a rooster or have to buy fertile eggs from elsewhere.

Even though roosters can sometimes be a nuisance, they actually serve a useful purpose in a chicken flock. Roosters naturally form their own group of hens, and their presence helps keep your flock together when you let them roam outside the coop. You won't have to worry about your hens wandering too far from each other with a rooster around! While it's true that chickens still like to explore and forage, having a rooster adds an extra layer of protection and helps maintain cohesion within the flock. So, despite any occasional annoyances, having a rooster can be quite handy for keeping your flock together.

Chickens require daily care and monitoring.

Raising chickens is not a part-time hobby – your birds will need attending to several times per day. At least once per day, you will need to feed and water the hens and collect any eggs. Depending on your setup, you may also need to let them out into their run in the morning and shut them securely into the coop at night.

Everything wants to eat a chicken.

It's worth noting that chickens are a popular target for predators, and everything from raccoons to hawks will try to make a meal out of your chickens if given the opportunity. You can take every step possible to protect your chickens and keep them safe and still potentially lose some birds to a hungry predator.

THE BENEFITS OF RAISING CHICKENS

The good news is that chicken keeping isn't all hard work and expense. Otherwise, none of us would do it! There are some advantages to keeping chickens that reach far beyond a regular supply of eggs and meat:

A constant supply of manure.

Everything you feed your chickens comes out as manure, a highly fertile byproduct that can be a fabulous fertilizer! The manure and litter from your chicken coop can be a great soil amendment if composted properly. However, it's important to be mindful of the potential risks associated with handling and disposing of chicken manure. More on this to come.

Chickens make wonderful pets.

Many people underestimate the intelligence and personality traits of chickens – you'll soon be hooked on watching them just going about their normal daily routine! Chickens are easy to tame and love hanging out with humans, making them great backyard pets.

Eggs, eggs, eggs!

Most people raise chickens because they want a regular supply of fresh eggs, and a happy, healthy backyard flock will provide you with these in abundance! Your eggs even come with a natural coating to preserve freshness, meaning they do not need to be refrigerated. Unrefrigerated they last 2 weeks, and 3 months once you do refrigerate.

QUESTIONS TO ASK YOURSELF BEFORE GETTING CHICKENS

Before leaping into the world of chickens, we have a few final questions you should consider first. By answering these honestly, you will be thoroughly prepared for any issues or problems that may arise along the way, helping to get you started on a lifetime of happy chicken rearing!

Do you have space?

Chickens need adequate space to move around, exercise, and forage for food. Consider the size of your yard or garden, and ensure it's large enough to accommodate a coop and a run for your chickens.

You will need a coop to provide your chickens with a safe and secure place to lay eggs, and roost. The coop should be large enough to accommodate your chickens comfortably, with plenty of ventilation and natural light.

Can you keep them safe?

Chickens are vulnerable to a variety of predators, including foxes, coyotes, hawks, raccoons, and even neighborhood dogs. Make sure that your coop and run are secure and predator-proof.

What will you do when they stop laying eggs?

While chickens can live for up to 10-12 years, they don't lay eggs consistently throughout their lives. Be prepared for the possibility that you may need to care for non-laying chickens in the future.

Can you afford it?

There are some initial start-up costs involved in raising chickens, such as purchasing or building a coop, feeders, and waterers, as well as ongoing costs, such as feed and veterinary care. Depending on the cost of chicken feed, it may be that you cannot produce eggs any cheaper than ones bought from the store. Later in the book, we will share some money-saving tips.

Who will take care of your chickens if you go on vacation?

Consider who will take care of your chickens if you go on vacation or need to be away for an extended period of time. Make sure that you have a trusted friend or neighbor who is willing and able to care for your chickens while you're away.

What will you do if one of your chickens gets sick or injured?

It's important to have a plan in place in case one of your chickens gets sick or injured. Are you prepared to provide veterinary care for your chickens, or do you have a local vet who is experienced in treating poultry?

If one of your cute fuzzy chicks turns out to be a rooster, what will you do?

Rearing chicks from your backyard hens may seem like a tempting prospect, but bear in mind that a good portion of those chicks will likely turn out to be roosters. Too many roosters in one location can cause significant problems, as they will fight for territory and can injure each other. Rehoming roosters is not always easy, as most other chicken owners have the same problem! This means you need to face the prospect of culling unwanted roosters if you cannot find them a new home.

SUMMARY

We hope this chapter has provided you a good overview of raising backyard chickens and the importance of being prepared, informed, and responsible when owning and caring for these wonderful animals.

We cannot emphasize enough the importance of checking local laws and regulations and understanding the needs of chickens before you commit to purchasing some new hens. By thoroughly doing your homework, you'll stand the best possible chance of rearing a happy, productive flock of backyard chickens.

So, you've done your research, and you're confident that you can provide everything your chickens need to give them a happy home; what is the next step?

You get to go chicken shopping, of course! In the next chapter, we will take an in-depth look at the most common and popular chicken breeds around the world, to help you decide the right type of chickens to purchase for your backyard flock.

2

NOT ALL CHICKENS ARE BORN THE SAME

*F*un fact – there are around four times as many chickens as humans on this planet! It is estimated that there are over 25 billion chickens currently on earth, with more than 500 chicken breeds and varieties among their population.

It is clear from these statistics that many people want to rear chickens, and these birds are a valuable commodity and essential food source all around the world. Not only do chickens provide fresh eggs and fertilizer for your garden, but they also make wonderful pets and are great for teaching children about responsibility and animal care.

But with so many different chicken breeds and varieties to choose from, how do you know which one is right for you?

The key is to choose a breed of chicken that matches your needs and preferences, whether that be egg-laying ability, meat production, or simply a striking appearance.

In this chapter, we'll explore some of the most popular chicken breeds and their characteristics, so you can make an informed decision and select the perfect chickens for your backyard flock.

We'll also cover topics such as egg-laying frequency, meat yield, temperament, cold and heat tolerance, and more, so you can choose the right chicken breed to suit your needs. So, whether you're looking for chickens that produce a steady supply of eggs for your family or chickens that are ideal for meat production, we've got you covered!

HOW TO CHOOSE THE PERFECT BREED OF CHICKEN

When choosing the perfect breed of chicken, it is important to consider factors such as why you want to keep chickens, the climate of the area where you live, the amount of space you have available, and your level of experience in chicken keeping.

The best place to start is to consider your goals – do you want chickens for eggs, meat, or both? This is the most important factor influencing the type of chickens you should purchase. Hens that are bred specifically to lay eggs do not make good meat chickens, and vice versa.

Here we've listed some of the most common and popular chicken breeds to suit a wide variety of situations. However, this is by no means an exclusive list, and there are many more fabulous breeds of chicken out there to choose from! But whatever type of chicken you opt for, remember that attributes such as hardiness and personality traits are equally, if not more, important than appearance.

BEST CHICKEN BREEDS FOR EGG PRODUCTION

When it comes to choosing chickens for egg production, some breeds are better suited than others. Factors that influence egg production include genetics, diet, and environmental conditions.

Chickens that have been selectively bred for high egg production will lay more eggs than breeds that have not. These types of chickens are known as "egg-layers" and are often smaller in size than meat breeds. However, high egg production can come at a cost, as these chickens may be more prone to health issues and have a shorter lifespan than less productive hens. Good egg layers are also less likely to go broody, so they are not always the best choice if you want to rear chicks.

If keeping your family supplied with fresh eggs is your priority, the best place to start is with one of these highly productive breeds:

- Leghorn: This breed is one of the most prolific egg layers, with hens capable of laying up to 280 white eggs per year. They have a somewhat skittish temperament and are better suited to warmer climates.

- Sussex: These chickens are known for being good layers of large, brown eggs, with hens capable of laying up to 250 eggs per year. They have a gentle disposition and are good foragers.

- Australorp: This breed is known for its consistent egg production, with hens capable of laying up to 250 brown eggs per year. They are also known for being good mothers and for their friendly personalities.

It's worth bearing in mind that egg production can vary widely within a breed and is also affected by factors such as diet and environment. However, the breeds listed above are generally known for being good egg layers and are excellent choices for backyard chicken keepers looking to maximize their egg yield.

BEST CHICKEN BREEDS FOR DIFFERENT COLORED EGGS

Some chicken breeds are famous for their unusually colored eggs, and many backyard chicken keepers like to keep several chicken breeds to get eggs of several different colors. Although the contents of the eggs all taste pretty much the same, there are some advantages to having differently colored eggs.

If you want to sell your surplus eggs, many customers like to buy eggs with unusual coloring. This can help you find a niche in the market and may even mean you can charge slightly more for your eggs.

Another advantage to different colored eggs is that children love them – this can be a great way to encourage your kids to eat your delicious home-grown produce!

So, if you're looking for hens that lay unusual eggs, here are some of our top recommendations:

- Ameraucana: These chickens lay blue or green eggs and have distinctive beards and muffs on their faces. They are known for being good layers and for their friendly personalities.

- Araucana: Similar to Ameraucanas, Araucanas also lay blue or green eggs but have no tail and often have tufts of feathers on their cheeks. They are a hardy breed that does well in cold climates.

- Maran: These chickens lay dark brown eggs that can range from a rich chocolate color to almost black. Marans are known for their calm temperament and are good foragers.

- Welsummer: Known for their large size and friendly personality, Welsummer chickens lay eggs with a deep, reddish-brown color.

- Easter Egger: This variety of hen is popular among backyard chicken keepers for its ability to lay eggs in a wide range of colors, including blue, green, pink, and even olive. The Easter Egger is not recognized as a breed by the American Poultry Association, but that hasn't stopped it from becoming one of the most-kept chickens in the U.S.!

- Cream Legbar: These chickens lay blue or green eggs and are known for their striking appearance, with a crest of feathers on their heads and a distinctive upright stance.

Keep in mind that egg color can vary within a breed, depending on factors such as age and diet, so you may not always get eggs that are the same shade. But overall, the breeds listed above are known for producing eggs that add a fun and unique touch to your breakfast table!

BEST CHICKEN BREEDS FOR MEAT PRODUCTION

Although rearing chickens for meat is not to everyone's liking, many chicken owners prefer to rear their own birds from meat rather than purchase it from the store. It is also undoubtedly true that home-reared chicken meat is tastier than mass-produced commercial chicken and healthier for us too.

Before considering the best types of chicken to rear for the table, we need to explain how the meat industry has evolved to produce the maximum meat in the fastest time with the minimum input. To achieve this goal, most commercial chicken farms rear hybrid chicks for meat – these are carefully selected crossbreeds, but the origins are often a closely guarded secret.

These hybrids grow incredibly quickly, and some can be ready for the table in as little as 6 weeks! In contrast, most heritage chicken breeds need at least 20 weeks before they are ready for consumption.

If you want to raise chickens for meat, you may be interested in purchasing hybrid chicks for a quicker return on your investment. However, it's worth noting that these chicks need indoor housing for the first two weeks of their lives. Because of this, they will only have about a month to roam outdoors and search for nourishing weeds and grubs before you process them. They are much different than heritage breeds that live a natural lifecycle.

Also, most hybrid meat chicks cannot be kept until adulthood to produce more chicks for two important reasons. Firstly, they may become so heavy that they die before they reach adulthood. They often can't even stand for long since they've gotten so plump in such a short time. Secondly, any eggs they do produce will not be true to their hybrid type and are unlikely to hatch chicks that are useful for meat production.

As we're all about raising chickens here, buying a batch of chicks from the hatchery every 6 weeks doesn't seem quite right! We like our chickens to grow at a normal, healthy rate and enjoy life outside as much as possible before they end up on the dinner table. We also like to raise chicks from our own hens to rear for meat, which is not possible with fast-growing hybrids.

If you're on the lookout for fast-growing hybrid chicks, the most widely available types are the Red Ranger, Cornish Cross, or Cornish Roaster. But if, like us, you prefer the idea of rearing traditional heritage chicken breeds for meat, the best place to start is with one of the following breeds:

- Jersey Giant: These chickens are one of the largest chicken breeds, with hens weighing up to 10 pounds and roosters up to 13 pounds. They have a good meat-to-bone ratio and are known for their flavorful meat.

- Brahma: This breed of chicken is also very large, with hens weighing up to 10 pounds and roosters up to 12 pounds. Their meat is described as rich and slightly sweet, and it is particularly juicy and tender.

- Cochin: These chickens are known for their large size and good meat production, with hens weighing up to 8 pounds and roosters up to 11 pounds. They have plump, juicy breast meat, which is prized for its tender texture.

- Bresse: Originating from France, the Bresse is smaller than the other meat birds on our list, weighing around 5-7 pounds when mature. However, the meat of these birds is considered to be a delicacy and is highly sought after.

Keep in mind that meat production is influenced by a

variety of factors, including genetics, diet, and environment. These breeds are known for their meat-producing qualities, but it is always a good idea to do additional research to ensure you choose the right breed for your specific needs.

BEST DUAL-PURPOSE CHICKEN BREEDS FOR EGG & MEAT PRODUCTION

Now this is our favorite category of chickens – breeds that can be reared for both egg and meat production! These are a great option if you want to raise chicks from a broody hen, as any roosters can be raised for meat and hens kept for future egg production.

Because dual-purpose chicken breeds are not quite so intensively bred for one purpose or another, they tend to be healthier chickens with fewer health problems. So, even though they may produce less in terms of eggs and meat, they are often easier and cheaper to keep.

Here are some of the best dual-purpose chicken breeds to choose from:

- Rhode Island Red: For backyard chicken keepers, the Rhode Island Red is a popular breed choice due to its ability to lay up to 260 brown eggs per year. This breed will grow to a reasonable size for meat production, with roosters weighing up to 8.5 pounds.

- Plymouth Rock: If you're looking for a dual-purpose chicken breed, the Plymouth Rock is an excellent option. Hens can lay up to 200 brown eggs annually, and their docile personality makes them a good choice for backyard chicken keeping. On average, Plymouth Rock roosters can weigh between 7 and 9 pounds when fully grown, and they are highly sought after for their tender meat.

- Orpington: This breed is a great dual-purpose option, with hens capable of laying up to 180 brown eggs per year and roosters growing to a large size for meat production. They have a good meat-to-bone ratio and are known for their flavorful meat.

- Wyandotte: This breed is a dual-purpose option, with hens capable of laying up to 200 brown eggs per year and roosters growing to a good size for meat production. They have a plump breast and are prized for their rich and tender meat.

Again, keep in mind that the egg and meat production of a chicken can vary based on several factors, including genetics, diet, and environment. These breeds are generally known for their dual-purpose qualities, but it's always a good idea to do additional research to find the best breed for your specific needs.

BEST CHICKEN BREEDS FOR COLD CLIMATES

Most chickens are relatively hardy and can cope better with colder temperatures than you might expect. However, if you live in an area where the winters are particularly harsh, choosing the right breed is crucial to ensure your chickens can thrive. Some chicken breeds have been specifically adapted to cope with harsh winter conditions, while others may struggle or even perish in colder weather.

Chickens with dense, fluffy feathers are better able to retain body heat and stay warm in colder temperatures.

Breeds with a thick undercoat of downy feathers and longer, coarser feathers on the outer layer are ideal for cold climates.

Larger chicken breeds tend to have a better ability to regulate their body temperature in colder weather. This is because they have a higher body mass-to-surface area ratio, which means they can produce and retain more body heat than smaller breeds. So, consider choosing larger breeds for cold climates.

The comb type is also important when selecting chicken breeds for cold climates. Chickens with smaller, less pronounced combs are better suited for cold climates, as larger combs are more prone to frostbite. Look for breeds with a pea comb or a small single comb, as these are less likely to be affected by cold weather.

The following breeds are known for their hardiness and are more likely to thrive in cold climates:

- New Hampshire: These chickens are a good choice for those looking for a dual-purpose bird that does well in cold climates. New Hampshire hens are capable of laying up to 200 brown eggs per year, and the roosters grow to a good size for meat production.

- Chantecler: This breed was specifically developed in Canada to do well in cold climates. They have a small comb and thick feathers and are known for their cold hardiness.

- Buckeye: The Buckeye chicken is known for its hardiness, versatility, and attractive appearance. They have a rich mahogany color and a pea comb, and their large size means they are better adapted to cope with colder climates.

Remember, while these breeds are known for doing well in cold weather, providing proper housing and care is crucial to ensure their health and well-being during the winter months.

BEST CHICKEN BREEDS FOR HOT CLIMATES

Raising chickens in hot climates can also be a challenge, as high temperatures can cause heat stress, dehydration, and other health issues. Choosing chicken breeds that are well adapted to hot weather can help ensure the birds' health and productivity. When choosing chicken breeds for hot climates, there are some key characteristics to look for.

Chickens with lighter, looser feathers are better suited to hot climates, as they allow for better air circulation around the bird's body, which helps to dissipate heat.

Large, heavy combs can be a disadvantage in hot weather, as they can trap heat and increase the risk of heat stress. Breeds with smaller, less pronounced combs are better suited to hot climates.

Smaller chicken breeds tend to be better suited to hot climates, as they produce less body heat and require less water to cool themselves down.

If you live in an area prone to long, hot summers, the following breeds are worth considering:

- Minorca: These chickens are known for their ability to tolerate heat well. They have a slender body shape and a large comb and wattles that help them dissipate heat.

- Ancona: This breed is also known for its ability to tolerate heat well. They have a slender body shape and a small comb and wattles, which helps them regulate their body temperature in hot weather.

- Fayoumi: These chickens have a slender body shape and a small comb and wattles, which helps them regulate their body temperature in hot weather.

Remember, while these breeds are known for their ability to do well in hot climates, it's important to provide proper housing, shade, and access to fresh water to ensure their health and well-being during the summer months.

BEST BANTAM CHICKEN BREEDS

Bantam chicken breeds are miniature versions of standard chicken breeds, and they can be great for backyard flocks due to their small size and often friendly personalities. Here are some fun and quirky bantam chicken breeds to consider:

- Cochin Bantam: These chickens are fluffy due to their feathered legs and abundant feathers. They are docile and make great pets.

- Silkie Bantam: Silkies are known for their soft feathers and gentle personalities. They are popular as pets and can be great brooders for hatching eggs.

- Sebright Bantam: Sebrights are friendly and active birds with a unique, laced feather pattern and upright tail feathers.

- Pekin Bantam: These chickens are miniature versions of the standard Pekin breed. Their calm and friendly temperament makes them great for backyard flocks.

- Dutch Bantam: Dutch Bantams are small and active birds with a variety of color patterns. They have friendly and curious personalities.

While bantams are very cute, they have different egg and meat production capabilities than their standard-sized counterparts. Before falling for that cute fluffy chicken at the store, it is important to research their individual characteristics, care requirements, and suitability for your needs before adding them to your flock.

LIFE CYCLE AND CONSIDERATIONS FOR BUYING CHICKENS

So, you've figured out the optimum number of chickens for your backyard and have decided which breeds would be best for you. The next big decision you need to make is whether to buy fertile eggs, chicks, or fully-grown birds!

Before making this choice, it pays to understand a little more about the life cycle of a chicken. We all know that chickens come from eggs, but a backyard chicken keeper needs to know a little bit more than that.

Here's a brief outline of the different life stages of a domesticated chicken:

Egg Fertilization

Eggs are fertilized when a rooster mates with a hen. Hens

without a rooster will still lay eggs, but they will not be fertilized and cannot develop into chicks.

After mating, sperm from the rooster travels up the hen's oviduct and fertilizes the egg as it is released. Once fertilized, an embryo forms inside the egg. This process takes about 21 days and involves the growth of various organs and features, such as the beak, eyes, and feathers.

It is possible to buy freshly laid fertilized eggs, which you can hatch either under a broody hen or in an incubator. This can be a good way to get a particularly unusual breed of chicken, as fertilized eggs can be shipped anywhere in the country using an overnight courier.

Hatching

After 21 days, the egg hatches, and a chick emerges. At first, the chick is covered in downy feathers and is completely dependent on its mother or you for warmth and food.

Chicks are available to purchase from hatcheries, as young as one day old, and they are often sent in the mail! Again, this can be a good way to get rare or unusual breeds of chickens. Some hatcheries can also guarantee the gender of your chicks, which is ideal if you want to avoid getting too many roosters.

Pullet

At around 6 weeks old, the chick becomes a pullet and begins to grow their adult feathers. It will be less dependent on its mother and can be moved into the main coop at this stage. Buying pullets is a good option if you don't have anywhere to hatch eggs or raise chicks.

Adult

By around 20-24 weeks, the pullet becomes a fully-grown hen or rooster. Hens can lay eggs at this point and are normally sold as 'point of lay' chickens. Many meat birds are culled at this age, particularly unwanted roosters.

SHOULD YOU PURCHASE CHICKENS OR EGGS?

When deciding to buy chickens, there are several age options to consider. Each option has its advantages and disadvantages, and it is important to understand what they are before deciding.

Fertilized eggs are the cheapest option, and they offer the opportunity to hatch your own chicks at a very low cost, particularly if you have a broody hen. Just remember there's no guarantee regarding the gender of your chicks, and it typically takes several months before they reach maturity and can actively contribute to your flock.

Day-old chicks are easy to obtain and offer the opportunity to raise chickens from a young age. When buying day-old chicks, you will need a heated brooder to keep them in, and they may be more expensive than fertilized eggs.

Pullets or young birds may be a good option if you want chickens that can start laying eggs sooner, and they are easier to care for than day-old chicks. They also tend to be cheaper than adult birds but more expensive than day-old chicks.

Point-of-lay birds are a great option if you want eggs as soon as possible, as they should start to lay soon after purchase. Because they are older, point-of-lay hens tend to be the most expensive option. It can also be difficult to find specific breeds of adult hens in some areas.

Another good option is to take on some rescue hens from a commercial chicken farm. This is a lovely way to give a home to a bird in need who may never have experienced life outside. Many rescue hens go on to lay eggs for several years to come, while others may have very poor egg production, making this option a bit of a gamble!

Breed Selection Chart

Breed Selection Map!

SUMMARY

Selecting the right chicken breeds for your flock is a critical first step in starting your backyard chicken operation. The breed you choose will determine the quality and quantity of eggs, the flavor and texture of meat, and how well your chickens will thrive in your climate. By considering factors such as temperament, egg production, and adaptability to local weather conditions, you can choose breeds that will provide you with the greatest benefit and be happy in your backyard!

Once you have chosen your chicken breeds, the next step is to prepare a suitable home for them. In the next chapter, we will explore the various factors to consider when building a chicken coop, including the size and design of the coop, how to keep it clean, and the importance of proper ventilation.

We will also discuss how to build a safe and secure outdoor run for your flock, as well as the logistics involved in rearing free-range hens. So, let's dive into the world of chicken housing and management!

3

IN THE COOP, WE GO

*I*n this chapter, we're going to discuss the ideal chicken housing, how to prepare the chicken coop, and much more. Providing and maintaining the perfect chicken coop and run is the key to keeping your new flock healthy, happy, and as productive as possible.

However, just for fun, let's start by busting some common myths about chickens that might surprise you!

MYTH #1: CHICKENS ARE ALL THE SAME

This is definitely not true! Chickens have their own individual personalities and behaviors, just like people or other animals. Some chickens are friendly and outgoing, while others are more reserved or shy. Some chickens are curious and adventurous, while others are content to stay in one place. Even in a group of identical hens, it can be easy to identify certain ones through their quirky little personality traits.

MYTH #2: ALL CHICKENS ARE GIRLS

Another common myth is that all chickens are females. In reality, chickens come in both male and female varieties, known as roosters and hens, respectively. Roosters have larger combs and wattles and are typically more colorful than hens. Many people only keep hens, which may be the reason for this very odd myth.

MYTH #3: ALL ROOSTERS ARE MEAN AND AGGRESSIVE

This is a stereotype that is not always true. While some roosters can be aggressive, especially during mating season, many are calm and docile and can become very tame. Our rooster is so friendly that he follows us around the yard, waiting to be petted! If you want to keep a rooster, it's important to choose a breed known for its calm temperament.

MYTH #4: CHICKENS CAN CHANGE THEIR GENDER

This is a complete myth. Chickens, like all birds, are born with a specific sex determined by their genetics. Someone can identify the gender of a chicken by examining its physical characteristics, such as the size and shape of its comb and wattles and the presence or absence of spurs (which only males have).

MYTH #5: CHICKENS ARE UNINTELLIGENT BIRDS WITH TINY BRAINS.

Contrary to popular belief, chickens are actually surprisingly intelligent creatures. They can recognize and remember over 100 different individuals and can navigate complex social hierarchies within their flock. Studies have shown that chickens can perform tasks that require problem-solving, such as finding food hidden in a puzzle or using tools to access food.

MYTH#6: CHICKENS WILL ONLY LAY EGGS IF A ROOSTER IS PRESENT

While a rooster is necessary for fertilization, hens will lay eggs regardless of whether or not a rooster is present. If you're not interested in breeding chickens, you don't need a rooster in your flock.

Now that we've busted a few myths let's move on to the important topic of chicken housing!

WHY DO CHICKENS NEED A COOP AND A RUN?

You may have seen many different types of chicken housing systems, but they all tend to have two things in common – a coop for the chickens to sleep in and an outdoor area for them to roam around in. This outdoor area is usually referred to as a run.

Theoretically, it is possible to keep chickens in a large coop without access to a run, but this limits their opportunities to carry out normal behavior such as foraging, scratching, and dust bathing. We want our hens to be happy and live natural lives, so in our opinion, an outdoor area is essential!

There are several ways in which you can provide an outdoor area for your chickens:

- A coop with a small enclosed run attached that you can move from area to area (this is often called a chicken tractor, as they clear your ground for you at the same time!)

- A larger, permanent outdoor run, often with a hatch leading to the chicken coop that can be closed at night.

- Free-range chickens are allowed to roam over a larger area that is not securely fenced, returning to the coop at night.

The first two options are the most convenient for most backyard chicken keepers. Although free-range chickens aim to mimic the lifestyle of wild chickens, this method has several drawbacks! We'll take a look at the pros and cons of free-range chickens in more detail later on.

Whichever setup you choose, your hens are going to need a coop. This is where they will roost, lay their eggs, and often hang out during the day. So, let's figure out how to build the perfect home for your new hens!

PREPARING THE CHICKEN COOP

As discussed in the first chapter, the most important aspect to consider is if your coop will be large enough for your new flock. Don't be tempted to squash too many hens into a small coop – these birds like their personal space when it comes to bedtime.

You will need to provide at least 2-3 square feet of indoor

space per chicken inside the coop. The coop should be tall enough to allow the birds to stand up straight and move around comfortably and be roomy enough for them to fly up to their roosting bars at night.

So, you've got the size of your structure figured out, but what's next? Well, it's time to get building! Here we have a detailed guide on how to build a safe and sturdy chicken coop, including some of the essential design features you should include along the way.

TIPS FOR BUILDING A SAFE AND STURDY DIY CHICKEN COOP

Although you're probably ready to start building straight away, it pays to spend a little time researching and planning your project first. This will help the build go smoothly and ensure you include all the elements your chickens need in their new home. There are a lot of different plans to choose from, so let's do our best to make an informed decision.

Location

Choose a location that is well-drained and provides good ventilation. Avoid low-lying areas that may become wet and muddy. To help keep your feathered friends safe, do not build the coop too close to trees or bushes that could provide predators with easy access.

Flooring

The key to a good chicken coop floor is to choose a material that is easy to clean, cannot harbor parasites, and is predator-proof. There are several flooring options for a chicken coop, each with its own advantages and disadvantages. Here are some of the most common options:

- Dirt: Dirt floors are the most natural and cost-effective option. They allow chickens to scratch and peck, which is an important natural behavior. However, dirt floors can become muddy and difficult to clean and may not provide adequate protection against predators or parasites.

- Concrete: Concrete floors are durable and easy to clean, making them popular for commercial chicken houses. However, concrete can be hard on chickens' feet and may require additional insulation to keep the coop warm. A layer of wood shavings on a concrete floor is a good option.

- Gravel: Gravel floors provide good drainage and can help prevent mud and moisture buildup. However, they may be uncomfortable for chickens to walk on and require a layer of bedding or sand for insulation.

- Wood: Wood floors provide good insulation and are comfortable for chickens to walk on. However, they can be difficult to clean and may harbor parasites or bacteria if not properly maintained.

PREDATOR PROTECTION

If you can, elevate the coop at least 1 foot off the ground to prevent predators from digging underneath. Alternatively, you can use wire mesh to enclose the bottom of the coop or choose a solid flooring option, such as concrete.

Doors

To ensure the hens are safe at night, most chicken owners have a coop with a solid door that can be closed at dusk and reopened in the morning. This hatch only needs to be large enough for the chickens to access, with a larger door at the back of the coop for you to enter when necessary to collect eggs and maintain the coop.

Latches

All doors and windows on the coop must have solid and sturdy latches to prevent predators from gaining access. Raccoons, in particular, are clever little critters and might terrorize your chickens if you don't take precautions to secure your coop well. If opening and closing the coop every day is going to be difficult due to time constraints, consider fitting a door that opens and closes automatically in response to daylight levels.

Nesting boxes & roosting bars

We'll talk about nesting boxes and roosting bars in more depth later on, but at this stage, you need to consider where they will be located. Nesting boxes should be in a quiet and secluded area of the coop, easily accessible for collecting eggs. Putting your roosting perches approximately 2 feet above the ground and in a separate area from the nesting boxes is also important.

Electricity

If you plan to use electricity in your coop, make sure a professional electrician does all wiring and that all outlets and fixtures are weather-resistant and safe for use around chickens. Electricity is not usually necessary in a chicken coop but can be helpful if you want to fit additional lighting.

Heat

The need for heaters in your chicken coop depends on factors like your climate, local weather, and the chicken breeds you're raising. Chickens are generally resilient in cold weather, but extreme cold can impact their health and egg production. While some chicken owners in places like Alaska manage without heaters, it's important to weigh your options carefully and prioritize safety.

In regions with harsh, cold winters, some chicken keepers use heaters or heat lamps to provide extra warmth. However, you need to be extremely careful because using the wrong heaters, improperly installed heaters, or faulty equipment can create a fire hazard and pose a risk to your chickens and your home. Many prefer alternatives like proper insulation, ventilation, and winterization techniques to keep chickens warm in colder climates.

If you do use heaters, please exercise extreme care. Electric heaters can be a potential fire hazard if not used correctly or if they come into contact with flammable materials in the coop. Safer heating options designed for coops are available and are equipped with features like automatic shut-off and protective guards. These heaters, such as radiant heat panels, infrared heaters, or ceramic heat emitters, offer consistent warmth without endangering the chickens.

Always follow the manufacturer's instructions for installing and using heating devices in the coop. If possible, seek professional installation. It's also a good idea to consult fellow chicken keepers in your area for advice tailored to your specific climate.

Most adult chickens do not need supplemental heat. In some cases a heated coop can prevent your chickens from adjusting to the cold, and it does more harm than good. Chicks need heat, but adult chickens generally don't.

Ventilation

Proper ventilation is essential for a healthy and comfortable living environment for chickens. Without adequate ventilation, moisture, dust, and ammonia can build up in the air, leading to respiratory problems and other health issues.

As a general rule of thumb, a chicken coop should have at least one square foot of ventilation per bird. This can be achieved through vents or windows near the roofline of the coop, which will allow hot air and moisture to escape while bringing in fresh air.

It's important to ensure that the ventilation openings are located high up on the walls of the coop to prevent drafts from blowing directly on the chickens. Additionally, it's a good idea to cover the openings with hardware cloth or other mesh to prevent predators from entering the coop.

In colder climates, you may need to adjust the amount of ventilation to prevent the chickens from getting too cold. You can do this by partially closing the vents or using insulation to cover them during the winter months. However, it's crucial to exercise caution if you have heaters in your coop. Depending on the type of heater you're using, there is a possibility of creating a hazardous environment for your chickens.

Clipping Wings

Some chickens are particularly flighty, so no matter how much you do to protect them from predators, your chickens could fly over your fence and get in trouble. Clipping a chicken's wings may seem like an odd practice, but it's common among poultry keepers, and it's not about stifling their dreams of flight; it serves several practical purposes for the chickens and their caretakers. Let's dig into why some chicken owners clip their birds' wings, the ethical considerations, and how to do it humanely.

One of the primary reasons for wing clipping is to prevent chickens from flying over fences and escaping their designated areas. In most situations, clipping your chickens' wings is crucial for their safety, as free-ranging chickens may wander into dangerous territory and become easy prey for predators or be fed something toxic by a well-meaning neighbor. By clipping their wings, owners can ensure their feathered friends stay within the confines of their secure coop, run, or in their backyards.

Now, let's address the ethics of wing clipping. Some argue it's a form of "chicken containment," restricting the birds' natural behavior. However, when done correctly and with care, it doesn't cause harm or discomfort to the chickens. One of our friends will only clip a chicken's wings if that bird has already been clipped at a young age, so they don't hinder a bird that has flown before. Think of it as analogous to trimming a pet's nails to prevent injury. Wing clipping is a responsible choice that helps protect the chickens while allowing them to lead happy and healthy lives.

When you decide to clip your chickens' wings, it's crucial to do it humanely. Always use sharp scissors or shears. It would make this process easier if someone gently held the chicken for you. You can gently hold the chicken in a towel for this. The goal is to trim the flight feathers that create lift. Trimming these feathers makes flying difficult but doesn't cause pain. Select the first ten or so primary flight feathers on one wing and trim them about halfway down their length. Be careful not to trim these feathers too short because you could hurt your feathered friend. It helps to use the tips of the secondary feathers as a guide, cutting the primary feathers just past where the tips of the second layer of feathers lie. Mirror the process on the other wing. Some people only clip one wing, but we recommend clipping the primary feathers on both wings. Remember that these feathers will grow back during the next molt, so this is a temporary measure. By following these guidelines, you can ensure your chickens stay safe while maintaining their overall well-being.

HOW MUCH DOES A CHICKEN COOP COST?

The cost of a chicken coop can vary widely depending on the size, design, and materials used. A simple, basic coop can be built for under $100, while a larger, more elaborate coop with multiple levels and custom features can cost several thousand dollars.

If you're handy with tools, you can save money by building your coop using plans or designs available online or in books. This will require the purchase of materials such as lumber, roofing materials, hardware, and wire mesh. The cost of these materials will depend on the size and complexity of the coop you're building and the cost of building materials in your area.

If you prefer to purchase a pre-made coop, prices can range from a few hundred to several thousand dollars. These coops are often made from higher-quality materials and may include features such as nesting boxes, roosting bars, and automatic feeders and waterers.

Ultimately, the cost of a chicken coop will depend on

your individual needs and preferences. If you're just starting out with backyard chicken keeping, a basic coop may be all you need to get started. As you become more experienced and your flock grows, you may decide to invest in a larger, more elaborate coop.

WHAT IS A CHICKEN RUN?

A chicken run is an enclosed outdoor space that provides chickens with a safe and secure area to move around and exercise. The run is typically fenced and can be made from a variety of materials, such as chicken wire, mesh, or wood.

A chicken run can be attached to a chicken coop or can be a standalone structure. It is designed to protect your chickens from predators, such as dogs, foxes, raccoons, and birds of prey. It also helps to keep the chickens from wandering too far from their coop and getting lost or injured.

In addition to providing safety and security, a chicken run allows chickens to engage in natural behaviors such as scratching for food, dust-bathing, and socializing with other chickens. It also helps to prevent chickens from damaging gardens or other areas of your yard.

WHERE SHOULD A CHICKEN RUN BE LOCATED?

When deciding where to locate a chicken run, several important factors must be considered to ensure your chickens' safety and well-being.

The run should be located in a well-drained area that is free from standing water. This helps to prevent the buildup of bacteria and parasites that can cause health problems for your chickens. Ideally, the run should be located near your home or in a visible area of your yard so predators are less likely to approach.

Choose an area for your chicken run that provides both sun and shade. This allows your chickens to regulate their body temperature and avoid overheating during hot weather.

Finally, the run should be located away from any areas where chemicals or other toxins are used, such as garden fertilizers or pesticides. These substances can be harmful to your chickens and should be avoided.

SEASONAL ADJUSTMENTS

Summer

Chicken coops can trap heat in the summer, so good ventilation is ideal. Give your chickens fresh bedding like straw in the coop and nesting boxes. Open the windows of your coop if you have them, and make sure they are predator-proof with hardware cloth screens. Also, try to add shade for the coop and run. Put a thin layer of straw in the sunny parts of the run to help keep your chickens from burning their feet.

Winter

On the flip side, coops need more insulation in the winter but don't completely close off the ventilation. You don't want a drafty coop in the winter, but you need some airflow to prevent ammonia buildup from chicken poop.

Straw, spray foam, and plywood are cheap ways to insulate the coop. Spray foam is a fast and easy way to seal up larger gaps and cracks in the walls and roof. Adding an extra layer of plywood to the walls and floor of the coop will also help significantly. The extra protection from wind will make the coop seem much warmer than it is outside.

Straw is another great insulator. Spread a thick layer in the coop and replace it when it gets wet. Another great tip is to give your birds alfalfa in the winter. It'll keep them entertained and give them something to peck and scratch at while providing a great source of vitamins, minerals, protein, and fiber.

STEP BY STEP GUIDE TO BUILDING YOUR CHICKEN COOP:

We understand that there is a lot to consider when building a chicken coop for the first time! To help take the guesswork out of the process, we've simplified it into eight easy-to-follow steps:

1. Pick your plan: Choose a coop design that meets your chickens' needs and fits within your budget and available space. There are many free and paid coop plans available online, or you can take a look at some friends' chicken coops for inspiration. We have included some plans for you at the end of the chapter!

2. Prepare the ground: Choose a level area of ground and clear it of any vegetation or debris. Level the ground if necessary and add a layer of sand or gravel to promote good drainage.

3. Put in the floor: Add a solid floor to your coop using plywood or similar materials. Use screws or nails to attach it to the frame. If your coop is elevated off the ground, you will probably be building the frame first.

4. Build your coop frame: Use pressure-treated lumber or PVC boards to build the frame of your coop. Use a circular saw or handsaw to cut the boards to the appropriate lengths and assemble them using screws or nails.

5. Add coop walls: Once the frame is complete, add walls to the coop using plywood or similar materials. Use a jigsaw, reciprocating saw, or handsaw to cut any openings for windows or vents.

6. Add your doors: Add a secure door to the coop using weather-resistant hinges and latches. Use a drill and screws to attach the hinges and latches to the frame.

7. Building nesting boxes and perches: Build nesting boxes and perches using plywood or similar materials. Nesting boxes should be at least a 12-inch by 12-inch square and located in a quiet and secluded area of the coop. Perches should be at least 2 feet off the ground and spaced at least 18 inches apart.

8. Accessorize the coop: Add any additional accessories you want, such as feeders, waterers, and lights. If you live in a colder climate that freezes in the winter, you may want a heated water container for those cold winter months. Places like Tractor Supply sell heated pet bowls that are safe to use. Another option is a heated base to put your water container on. Make sure all accessories are secure and safe for use around chickens.

MATERIALS & TOOLS NEEDED TO BUILD A CHICKEN RUN

Materials needed to build a chicken run may include:
- Pressure-treated lumber or metal posts
- Wire mesh or chicken wire
- Concrete mix
- Screws or nails
- Hinges and latches
- Post hole digger
- Staple gun or zip ties

Tools needed to build a chicken run include:
- Circular saw, reciprocating saw, or handsaw
- Drill
- Level
- Tape measure
- Hammer

STEP-BY-STEP GUIDE TO BUILDING A CHICKEN RUN

Building a chicken run doesn't have to be complicated or expensive. With some basic tools, materials, and a little bit of know-how, you can create a custom-made run that will meet the specific needs of your chickens and your backyard space. In this step-by-step guide, we'll walk you through the process of building a chicken run, from planning and design to construction and finishing touches.

1. Plan how big the chicken run should be: Consider the number of chickens you have, their size, and how much space they need to move around and forage. A good rule of thumb is to provide at least 10 square feet of space for each chicken in the run.

2. Set your posts: Use pressure-treated lumber or metal posts to set the perimeter of your chicken run. Space the posts about 6-8 feet apart, and use a post-hole digger to create holes that are at least 2 feet deep. Pour concrete around the posts to secure them in place.

3. Attach the wire fencing: Use wire mesh or chicken wire to enclose the perimeter of the run. Attach the wire fencing to the posts using staples or zip ties. Make sure the bottom of the fence is buried at least 6 inches underground to prevent predators from digging underneath.

4. Create your frame: Use pressure-treated lumber or PVC boards to create a frame for the roof of the run. Attach the frame to the posts using screws or nails.

5. Add a door: Create a secure door for the run using weather-resistant hinges and latches. Use a drill and screws to attach the hinges and latches to the frame.

ACCESSORIZING YOUR CHICKEN COOP AND RUN

Now you've got your chicken coop and run well underway, it is time to start adding in all the things that will keep your hens in top condition!

Food and water containers

When it comes to feeding and watering your backyard chickens, there are a variety of container options and styles to choose from. For waterers, you can choose between plastic or metal fountains, gravity-fed containers, or nipple-style waterers. Plastic and metal fountains are easy to fill and clean, while gravity-fed containers, like fonts or tanks, can be filled with a hose or bucket. Nipple-style waterers provide a consistent flow of clean water and help prevent water waste, but they require some installation.

For feeders, common options include plastic or metal troughs, hanging feeders, and treadle feeders. Troughs and hanging feeders are easy to fill and clean, while treadle feeders are designed to open only when a chicken steps on a foot pedal, which helps keep pests out of the feed.

You can also make your feeders and waterers using materials like PVC pipes, buckets, or plastic containers. These homemade options can be cost-effective and customized to your specific needs.

When selecting food and water containers for your chickens, it's important to consider factors like ease of cleaning and filling, durability, and protection from pests. It's also important to regularly clean and maintain your containers to prevent disease and ensure your chickens have access to clean and fresh food and water.

Scratching area

Chickens love to scratch and peck at the ground, so providing a designated scratching area is important. This can be an area filled with soil, sand or even a small patch of grass. Make sure it's big enough to accommodate all of your chickens.

Dust bath

Chickens also need to take dust baths to keep themselves clean and healthy. Provide a designated dust bath area, which can be filled with sand, dirt, or wood ash. You can even add some diatomaceous earth to the dust bath to help control parasites.

Sunning area

Like us, chickens need access to sunlight to produce vitamin D, which is essential for strong bones and overall health. Make sure your coop has a sunny area where your chickens can bask in the sun.

Foraging area

Chickens are natural foragers and need a designated area where they can search for food. You can create a foraging area by planting grass, clover, or other vegetation or scattering some scratch grains or mealworms for your chickens to find.

Hideouts and shelter

Chickens need a place to retreat and feel safe from predators. Provide some hiding places, such as bushes or wooden structures, as well as a sturdy shelter where they can stay dry and warm in bad weather.

SHOULD YOU RAISE FREE-RANGE CHICKENS?

A flock of free-range chickens sounds idyllic, but many who try this method end up eventually confining them to a run (ourselves included!). There are some great advantages to having free-range hens, but also some disadvantages that often outweigh the benefits.

Here are the main pros and cons of letting chickens roam free:

Advantages of free-range chickens

- Natural behavior: Chickens are natural foragers and enjoy pecking and scratching at the ground to find insects, worms, and plants. Free-range chickens have the opportunity to engage in these natural behaviors, which can improve their physical and mental health.

- Nutritious eggs: Free-range chickens have access to a wider variety of foods and nutrients, which can result in eggs that are more nutritious and flavorful.

- Cost savings: When chickens are allowed to roam free, they have the opportunity to find some of their own food, which can save on feed costs.

Disadvantages of free-range chickens

- Predators: Free-range chickens are more vulnerable to predators like foxes, coyotes, and hawks. If you live in an area with a lot of predators, keeping free-range chickens safe may be more difficult.

- Damage to plants and property: Chickens can cause damage to gardens, flower beds, and other areas of your property if they are allowed to roam free.

- Difficulty controlling where they go: Free-range chickens may wander onto your neighbor's property, which could lead to disputes or legal issues.

Ultimately, the decision to raise free-range chickens will depend on your individual situation and priorities. If you have the space and resources to safely allow your chickens to roam free, it can provide a variety of benefits. However, if you are concerned about the safety of your chickens or the potential damage they may cause, you may want to consider a more enclosed coop and run setup.

Our solution was to build a large run for our hens but then let them free-range for an hour or so before bedtime when we were there to supervise them. This seems to be working well for everyone involved so far and gives our hens the best of both worlds!

Super Cute Coop With Run Plan (6 chickens)

4'x8' Coop Plans (10-16 chickens)

Coop Plans From *'Ana White'*

Thirteen More Free Coop Plans From 'The Spruce'

SUMMARY

In conclusion, providing a safe and comfortable living environment is essential for keeping healthy and happy backyard chickens. From choosing the right type of coop to selecting the best food and water containers, there are many factors to consider when creating a suitable living space for your feathered friends.

Though building a coop and run is just the beginning. It's important to provide them with a balanced diet and plenty of fresh water to keep your chickens healthy and productive. In the next chapter, we'll explore the best types of feed for chickens and how to provide them with proper nutrition to keep them laying eggs, growing strong, and thriving.

Whether you're a beginner backyard chicken keeper or an experienced poultry enthusiast, learning how to feed your chickens properly is a crucial step in raising healthy and happy birds. So, let's dive in and discover the secrets to keeping your flock well-fed and content.

4

FEEDING CHICKENS

*C*hickens are wonderful creatures that offer many benefits to backyard farmers, from fresh eggs to natural pest control. As chickens are omnivores, they consume a wide variety of food, including grains, vegetables, fruits, and even insects and small animals. Spend some time watching a group of hens foraging, and you'll quickly realize how varied their tastes really are!

However, not everything that is safe for humans or other animals is suitable for chickens. In fact, some food can be toxic, leading to illness or even death. To keep your chickens healthy, happy, and productive, it is essential to be aware of what you can and cannot feed them. In this chapter, we'll explore the ins and outs of the chicken diet, including what to feed them, what to avoid, and how to balance their nutritional needs.

THE NUTRITIONAL NEEDS OF CHICKENS: UNDERSTANDING WHAT YOUR BIRDS REQUIRE

Like all animals, chickens have specific nutritional needs that must be met to maintain their health and well-being. Chickens are omnivores, meaning they eat food of both plant and animal origin.

While chickens can eat a wide variety of food, the bulk of their diet should consist primarily of a balanced feed that provides all the necessary nutrients – in other words, chicken feed. A good quality chicken feed should contain protein, carbohydrates, fats, vitamins, and minerals in the right amounts and proportions.

Protein is especially important for chickens as it is essential for growth, development, and egg production. Most chicken feeds have a protein content of around 16-18%, which is sufficient for most birds. However, if you have young chicks, laying hens, or birds with high energy requirements, you may need to choose a feed with a higher protein content.

Carbohydrates and fats are also crucial for chickens, providing energy and supporting metabolic processes. However, a diet that is too high in carbohydrates can lead to obesity and other health problems.

If you buy a sack of chicken feed formulated for your type of chickens – e.g., laying hens, young chicks, or meat birds – then you are already on the right track with their food source. But what if you want to add anything extra to their diet? After all, a great advantage to having chickens is their eagerness to tuck into our dinner table leftovers and kitchen waste!

A good rule of thumb is to stick to the 90:10 rule when it comes to chicken feed vs. treats. This means that around 90% of their daily diet should be nutritionally balanced chicken feed, with the remaining 10% reserved for treats or supplements.

So, while spoiling your birds with tasty snacks is tempting, treats should always be given in moderation and as part of a balanced diet. Too many treats can disrupt the nutritional balance of your birds' diet, leading to obesity, malnutrition, and other health issues.

But when it comes to chickens, what constitutes a 'treat,' and what foods can be incorporated as part of their main diet?

A treat is a food that is not nutritionally balanced and would cause health problems if fed in large quantities. For example, my hens adore eating bread, so they get a few leftover crusts from our kitchen now and again. In terms of nutrients, bread is high in carbohydrates and low in essential nutrients, so if I allowed my hens to eat as much bread as they wanted, they would soon become unhealthy and at risk of illness.

On the other hand, if a food is nutritionally balanced and adds value to the diet, it can be considered to be part of the daily feed rather than a treat. We frequently cook up rice, beans, and chopped vegetables to supplement our chicken feed, which helps keep costs down and adds variety to our hen's daily food intake.

CHICKEN FEED OPTIONS: EXPLORING THE DIFFERENT TYPES OF FEED AND TREATS

When starting out with rearing chickens, your first errand will probably be picking up a sack of chicken feed at the farm store. The simplest way to ensure your birds get a balanced diet is to ensure that this feed makes up at least 90% of their daily food intake, with the remainder consisting of extra treats.

Commercial feeds are the most popular and convenient option for most backyard chicken keepers. They are specially formulated to provide a balanced and complete diet for chickens and come in different types and formulations depending on your birds' needs. Some common types of commercial feeds include:

- Starter feed: high-protein feed for young chicks up to 8 weeks old

- Grower feed: lower-protein feed for chicks 8-16 weeks old

- Layer feed: high-calcium feed for laying hens

- All-purpose feed: a general-purpose feed for adult birds

- Organic feed: made with organic ingredients and free from synthetic additives

These feeds tend to come in two forms; pellets or whole grains. Both contain similar ingredients, but in pelleted feeds, they have been ground or mashed into a pulp and then formed into pellets. The advantage of pelleted feeds is that it prevents selected feeding, where the birds pick out their favorite grains from a mixed grain feed and leave the less tasty morsels.

In terms of the quantity of feed, it is advisable to follow the directions on the product to determine how much to feed your flock. The amount of feed you give your chickens will depend on their age, breed, and size. As a general rule, laying hens should have access to about ¼ to ½ pounds of feed per day. You can adjust the amount of feed based on your birds' appetites and growth.

In addition to commercial chicken feed, you can supplement your birds' diet with various herbs, vegetables, plants, and kitchen scraps. Some healthy options include:

- Fresh herbs such as parsley, basil, oregano, and thyme can add flavor and nutrients to your birds' diet.

- Leafy greens, including lettuce, spinach, and kale, are a good source of essential vitamins and minerals.

- Fruits such as apples, berries, and melons are a good source of antioxidants and fiber.

- Additional grains, like oats, wheat, and barley, can be fed in moderation as a source of carbohydrates.

- Protein-rich foods, including peas, mealworms, earthworms, and small insects, can be fed as a treat or supplement to boost your birds' protein intake.

Chickens also enjoy eating many of our dinner table leftovers and kitchen scraps, such as bread, cheese, cake, and cooked pasta. However, these are not nutritionally balanced foodstuffs and should only be fed in very limited amounts alongside commercially-produced chicken feed.

It is clear to see that there are many options for feeding your chickens, including commercial feeds, supplements, and homemade treats. Each type of feed has its own benefits and drawbacks and should be chosen based on your birds' specific needs. Supplementing your birds' diet with fresh herbs, vegetables, and scraps can provide additional nutrients and variety, but care should be taken to avoid feeding them harmful foods.

WHEN AND HOW TO FEED YOUR CHICKENS

So, you've got your chicken's daily food rations figured out, but when do you need to feed them? This will vary according to your circumstances, so there are a few options to consider.

You will notice that your chickens are at their hungriest first thing in the morning – this is because laying hens will eat much of their daily ration before midday, helping to ensure that they have the necessary energy and nutrients to lay eggs. Therefore, it's important to provide them with a large portion of their feed in the morning.

For the remainder of the day, your flock will browse the remaining food, as well as forage for tasty morsels such as insects, worms, and plants. I have frequently noticed that our hens like high-calorie, protein-rich food in the morning, but as the day goes on, they switch to eating plants, seeds, and herbs.

For hens kept in a smaller run with limited foraging opportunities, some additional feed may be required in the afternoon or evening. Another option is to provide constant access to food in a gravity feeder or hanging feeder, giving your chickens free choice of when to eat.

Although chickens love their food and have healthy appetites, they are not overly prone to obesity, so free-choice feeding is not normally a problem. However, you may find that local wildlife and even rodents develop a taste for your chicken food, which can become problematic.

Treats can be offered to hens by scattering them in the coop or placing them in a feeder. Take care to remove uneaten treats every evening to avoid attracting rodents.

Feeding treats to your flock by hand can be a fun way to make friends with your hens!

Clean water is vital for your hens' health, so make sure they always have access to it! You will notice that they drink a surprising amount of water. They dislike drinking warm water, so remember to refill the drinking station regularly with cool, fresh water on hot days. Put the watering station in the shade if possible.

If you're struggling to decide on a feeding routine for your flock, here is a sample feeding schedule for laying hens:

Morning: Give around half the daily ration of chicken feed to ensure your hens have the necessary energy and nutrients to lay eggs.

Afternoon: Give a quarter of the daily ration or a portion of homemade chicken feed, along with some treats.

Evening: Offer the remaining portion of feed to keep the hens full throughout the night. Remove any uneaten treats from the coop.

If you don't have time to feed your chickens three times a day, give them extra in the morning to browse throughout the day. Keep an eye on your chicken's appetites and adjust the amounts of feed accordingly – if they leave a lot of food uneaten, you are likely feeding too much!

WHAT NOT TO FEED YOUR CHICKENS: A LIST OF FOODS AND SUBSTANCES TO AVOID

While chickens are omnivores and can eat a huge range of different foodstuffs, there are some foods and substances that are harmful or toxic to them. Here's a list of common foods to avoid giving to your chickens:

- Avocado pits and skins contain a toxin called persin, which is poisonous to chickens.

- Undercooked or dried beans contain a substance called phytohaemagglutinin (PHA), which can cause digestive upset and even death in chickens. To avoid this problem, beans should be thoroughly cooked and not fed to your birds in large quantities.

- Rhubarb leaves contain oxalic acid, which can be toxic to chickens if consumed in large amounts. It's best to avoid feeding rhubarb to your birds altogether and keep your hens well away from your vegetable plot if you are growing rhubarb.

- Moldy, rotten food can contain harmful bacteria and toxins that can make your chickens sick. Discard any spoiled food and avoid feeding it to your birds, and make sure to remove any uneaten treats from the coop if not eaten within a few hours.

- Chocolate contains theobromine, which can be toxic to chickens in large amounts. It's best to avoid feeding chocolate to your birds altogether.

- Potato peels contain solanine, which can be toxic to chickens in large amounts.

- Coffee and coffee grinds contain caffeine, which can be harmful to chickens in large amounts.

- Citrus fruit peels can contain harmful oils that can irritate your birds' digestive systems.

- Processed food contains high levels of salt, sugar, and preservatives, which can harm chickens. It's best to avoid feeding processed food to your birds and stick to natural, whole foods.

BALANCING YOUR CHICKENS' DIET: DIY CHICKEN FEED RECIPE

As a newly-fledged chicken keeper, you might be alarmed by the cost of chicken feed! Many people find that purchasing chicken feed can be even more expensive than buying eggs, especially in the early days when your point-of-lay hens are laying fewer eggs than you'd hoped.

The other issue with purchasing chicken feed is that you cannot always guarantee the quality of the ingredients. Unless you can source organic, GMO-free feed, you cannot be sure you are feeding your hens the highest quality feed. And, as most people keep chickens for the pleasure of eating fresh, healthy eggs and meat, it stands to reason that we want to feed them the very best!

While commercial chicken feed is a convenient and widely available option for chicken owners, making your own chicken feed has several advantages. By formulating a balanced feed that meets your chickens' specific nutritional needs, you can save money and ensure your birds get the best possible diet.

Chicken nutrition is a vast subject, and if you plan on making your own chicken feed, it pays to research this in more depth first. Any imbalance of nutrients can be hugely detrimental to your birds, so you may do more harm than good if the balance of ingredients is not quite right.

To formulate a balanced chicken feed, it's important to consider your birds' age and stage of development. Young chicks require more protein than adult birds, while laying hens require additional calcium to support egg production.

To get you started, here is a brief overview of the key components of a balanced chicken feed:

- 60% grains (such as wheat, corn, barley, or oats)
- 20% protein source (such as soybean meal, fish meal, or dried insects)
- 10% calcium source (such as ground limestone, crushed eggshells, or oyster shells)
- 5% seeds (such as flaxseed or sunflower seeds)
- 5% other ingredients (such as dried herbs, vegetables, or fruit)

To ensure that your chickens are getting all the nutrients they need, you may also need to add a vitamin and mineral supplement to their feed. These are available from most reputable farm stores and are a great way to ensure your hens get a balanced diet. If you are feeding a commercially-produced chicken feed, no additional supplements should be necessary unless a deficiency is diagnosed.

When making your own chicken feed, you will need some basic equipment, including a grain mill or grinder, a mixing bowl or container, and a measuring cup or scale. You can adjust the recipe based on your birds' specific needs and preferences, but it's crucial to ensure that their diet is well-balanced and provides all the nutrients they need to thrive.

If this method sounds too complex, I've come across another great way to bulk out your chicken feed, helping you save money without compromising on the quality of your hen's daily food intake.

To do this, I cook up a batch of kitchen scraps and vegetable garden waste, along with additional carbohydrates in the form of rice. Many farm stores sell sacks of dried rice intended for animal feed, which can be super cost-effective. A typical batch of cooked rice and veggies for my hens will include a blend of the following in a 50:50 mix with rice:

- Vegetable peelings – carrots, parsnips, beets, cucumber, zucchini, squash
- Leafy greens & brassicas – lettuce, spinach, leaf beets, collard greens, kale, broccoli
- Vegetable stalks – broccoli, celery, cauliflower
- Pea pods

To make this recipe, chop all the vegetables and pop them into a pan with 2 cups of water. Bring to a boil, add 1 cup of rice, and cook until the rice is soft. By cooking the rice with the vegetables, any nutrients that leak out into the water will be absorbed by the rice. A handful of lentils can also be added for an extra protein boost when needed, such as when your hens are molting.

The cooked rice and veggie mix is fed to our flock at lunchtime instead of their commercial chicken feed. This reduces our feed bill by around a third and makes excellent use of vegetable scraps that would otherwise end up in the compost bin.

ANOTHER SIMPLE RECIPE FOR CHICKEN FEED MADE FROM KITCHEN SCRAPS:

Ingredients:

- Kitchen scraps (vegetable peels, fruit trimmings, and leftover cooked food)
- Grains (rice, oats, barley, or corn)
- Legumes (lentils, chickpeas, or beans)
- Seeds (sunflower seeds or flaxseeds)

Instructions:

1. Collect Kitchen Scraps: Save vegetable peels, fruit trimmings, and leftover cooked food from your kitchen. Avoid using anything toxic or harmful to chickens, such as onions, garlic, chocolate, or citrus peels.
2. Prepare Grains and Legumes: Measure equal parts of grains (rice, oats, barley, or corn) and legumes (lentils, chickpeas, or beans).
3. Mix Ingredients: In a large container or bucket, combine the kitchen scraps with the grains and legumes in a 1:1 ratio. Mix well to ensure an even distribution.
4. Add Seeds: Sprinkle a small amount of seeds (sunflower seeds or flaxseeds) into the mix for added nutrients and healthy fats.

HOMEMADE CHICKEN TREATS: IDEAS FOR HEALTHY AND DELICIOUS SNACKS YOUR BIRDS WILL LOVE

While a balanced commercial feed is the mainstay of a chicken's diet, treats can be a great way to provide extra nutrition and variety to your flock. Homemade chicken treats are a great option because they are often healthier and more affordable than store-bought options. Here are some ideas for homemade chicken treats that your birds will love:

- Fresh herbs: Chickens love fresh herbs like parsley, basil, and mint. You can hang bunches of herbs in your coop or scatter them in your run for your birds to peck at.

- Vegetables: Most chickens love vegetables, especially leafy greens like kale, cabbage, and spinach. You can chop up vegetables into small pieces and mix them into your birds' feed or hang leafy greens in your coop for your birds to peck at. One of our friends suspends a cabbage in the run using a string, and the chickens enjoy pecking at it as it swings around.

- Fruits: Fruits like berries, melons, and grapes are a great source of vitamins and minerals for chickens. You can chop up fruits into small pieces and mix them into your birds' feed or hang slices of fruit in your coop for your birds to peck at.

- Homemade seed blocks: You can make your seed blocks by mixing birdseed with gelatin or peanut butter and molding it into a block shape. Once the block has set, you can hang it in your coop or run for your birds to peck at.

- Mealworms: Mealworms are a great source of protein for chickens. You can buy live or dried mealworms and scatter them in your run for your birds to eat.

When making homemade chicken treats, it's important to avoid foods that are harmful to chickens, like avocado, chocolate, and coffee grounds. It's also important to offer treats in moderation and to ensure that they do not make up more than 10% of your birds' diet. By offering your chickens healthy and delicious treats, you can help keep them happy, healthy, and entertained.

COMMON CHICKEN FEEDING MISTAKES: HOW TO AVOID THEM AND KEEP YOUR FLOCK SAFE

Feeding your chickens is an important part of their care, but it's important to avoid common feeding mistakes that can harm your flock. Here are some mistakes to watch out for:

- Overfeeding: Overfeeding your chickens can lead to obesity, which can cause health problems such as heart disease, egg binding, and reduced egg production. It's important to monitor your chickens' weight and adjust their feed accordingly. If they are frequently leaving uneaten food, you are most likely feeding them too much!

- Underfeeding: On the other hand, underfeeding can lead to malnourishment and poor egg production. This can be especially problematic if poor-quality feed is given or when weaker hens are bullied and cannot access food. Feed the best-quality chicken feed you can afford, and for larger flocks, provide several feeding stations to ensure all hens have equal access.

- Giving too many treats: Treats can be a fun way to supplement your chickens' diet, but giving too many treats can lead to nutritional imbalances and health problems. Remember, treats should make up no more than 10% of your chickens' diet.

- Not providing grit: Grit is essential for chickens to digest their food properly. If you're feeding your chickens whole grains or other large particles, make sure to provide some added grit so they can properly digest their food. Chickens need grit in their diet because it helps them mechanically break down food in their gizzard to digest it properly. Since chickens don't have teeth, the grit acts like tiny rocks in their stomach, helping to grind up the food so they can get all the nutrients from it.

TROUBLESHOOTING CHICKEN FEEDING ISSUES: HOW TO SOLVE PROBLEMS AND KEEP YOUR FLOCK HAPPY

Sometimes feeding your chickens can be difficult, and issues may arise. It's important to first rule out any health problems and then review your feeding routine to see if that could be the cause of the issue.

If your hens have suddenly stopped laying eggs or their egg production has decreased, it may be due to a lack of proper nutrition. Ensure that your hens receive adequate amounts of a balanced diet that includes enough protein and calcium and that they have access to fresh, clean water.

Obesity in chickens can lead to problems including decreased fertility, egg-binding, and prolapsed vent. Feeding too much food or the wrong type of food can quickly lead to obesity in hens. Reduce the amount of feed you're giving them and limit their treats to no more than 10% of their diet.

Chickens can also suffer from nutritional deficiencies if they aren't getting the right balance of nutrients. Ensure your chickens receive a balanced diet that includes all the necessary nutrients, and consider supplementing their feed with additional vitamins or minerals if necessary.

Some chickens can be picky eaters and may refuse certain foods, selecting only their favorite foods and leaving the rest. If you notice this, try offering a variety of different foods to see what your chickens prefer, and consider mixing in different feeds to make them more appealing. Alternatively, feed a pelleted feed to prevent selective feeding.

If your chickens are aggressive towards each other at feeding time, try providing multiple feeding stations so they can eat separately. You can also try scattering the feed on the ground so they have to forage for it, which helps reduce aggression. This also encourages natural behavior such as scratching and foraging.

SUMMARY

When you start raising backyard chickens, it's essential to keep in mind that their diet is vital to their health and well-being. By providing them with a balanced diet and avoiding harmful substances, you can help to ensure that your flock remains healthy and happy.

In the next chapter, we will be discussing common chicken health problems and how to deal with them. We will explore various health issues that chickens may face, such as respiratory problems, parasites, and egg-laying issues, and provide advice on how to prevent and treat these problems. Stay tuned for an informative and engaging chapter that will help you keep your flock in good health!

Get Clucking!

Nothing in life is more important than the ability to communicate effectively."

— GERALD R. FORD

It won't take you long to notice that chickens are very communicative. Unfortunately, they mostly only talk to each other, so until you've had your flock for a while and have started to decipher their sounds, you'll be none the wiser as to what they're saying.

A happy, healthy flock is usually loudest in the morning; if they're quiet, it's worth checking the coop to make sure nothing is amiss. You'll get to know the sound of an egg being laid by the staccato clucks made by the egg-layer, which build into a loud, triumphant call. You might even get to know when there's an air-bound predator overhead by the high-pitched shrieks, and if there's a threat on the ground, you'll hear a repetitive clucking sound.

Chickens let each other know what's going on. It helps the flock stay ahead of any danger, and it shows them where to look for threats. It's just like us giving directions or leaving reviews to let other people know what our experience was like with a place or a product.

I'd like to ask you to channel the community spirit of the chickens now to let other newbie chicken owners know where they can find the guidance they need to get started.

By leaving a review of this book, you'll send a call-out to new readers, much like the chickens calling out to the rest of the flock, to let them know where they can find what they're looking for.

Simply by letting other readers know how this book has helped you and what they'll find inside, you'll show them where they can find all the information they need to get started with raising their own flock.

Review link:

5

HEALTHY CHICKENS ARE HAPPY CHICKENS

*C*hickens are one of the most commonly farmed animals in the world and are a major source of food for millions of people. However, just like any other living creature, they are susceptible to a wide range of health problems that can have serious consequences for their well-being and productivity.

In fact, according to the USDA, poultry diseases cost the U.S. industry a massive $3 billion annually! And as a backyard chicken keeper, I know just how quickly disease can cause devastation amongst a well-loved flock. It stands to reason that understanding the common health issues that affect chickens and how to prevent or manage them is crucial for anyone interested in raising backyard chickens.

When it comes to chicken health, it's important to remember that although these birds are incredibly resilient, they are also susceptible to a range of illnesses and diseases. Unlike other animals, chickens tend to hide their symptoms well, making it difficult for their owners to identify an issue before it escalates. This is especially true since chickens are prey animals and have evolved to hide their weakness from predators. As a result, health problems in chickens can deteriorate quickly, leading to serious complications or even death.

Given the rapid progression of many chicken health problems, seeking veterinary advice as soon as possible is always the best course of action. A qualified veterinarian can help diagnose the issue and provide guidance on appropriate treatment options. Waiting too long to seek help can result in more severe symptoms and more complex treatment requirements, which can be costly and time-consuming.

In this chapter, we will cover the basic facts about the most common chicken disorders and diseases to help you recognize when your birds might be unwell.

COMMON CHICKEN EGG-LAYING ISSUES

Egg-laying disorders are relatively common among chickens and can have a significant impact on their overall health and productivity. It can be such a huge disappointment when you go to collect your eggs only to find that they are deformed or, even worse, that you have none at all! Some of the most common egg-laying disorders include:

- Egg Binding: This occurs when a hen is unable to lay an egg due to a blockage in the reproductive tract. The hen may appear lethargic, have difficulty walking, and may even strain to lay an egg. This condition is a medical emergency and requires immediate veterinary attention.

- Soft-shelled Eggs: Hens may lay soft-shelled or shell-less eggs, which can be caused by a lack of calcium or a poor diet. This can be resolved by ensuring that hens have access to a balanced diet and calcium supplements. Soft-shelled eggs are also common in young point-of-lay hens when they lay their first few eggs.

- Egg Eating: Hens may start to eat their own eggs or eggs from other hens, which can be caused by a lack of calcium, boredom, or overcrowding. This can be addressed by providing a nutrient-rich diet and increasing the amount of space available to the hens. Collecting the eggs regularly can also keep them safe from egg-eating hens.

- Decreased Egg Production: Hens may stop laying eggs or produce fewer eggs due to stress, disease, or age. This can be managed by ensuring that hens have access to a comfortable environment, a balanced diet, and regular veterinary care. It is also common for hens to lay less during the winter months and when they are molting.

SKIN AND FEATHER PROBLEMS IN CHICKENS

Chickens are susceptible to various skin and feather problems that can impact their health and well-being. One common problem is cuts and peck marks, often caused by fights among chickens or sharp edges in the coop or run. These wounds can become infected and should be treated promptly with antiseptic ointment or spray. In severe cases, a veterinarian may need to clean and stitch the wound.

Foot Problems

One of the most common foot problems in chickens is bumblefoot, a bacterial infection that causes swelling, redness, and pain on the bottom of the foot. Bumblefoot is typically caused by cuts or scrapes on the foot and can be prevented by providing a clean and dry living environment and providing perches with appropriate size and texture. Treatment for bumblefoot may include antibiotics and surgery in severe cases.

Molting

If you start to see feathers everywhere in your coop in the fall, don't immediately panic! Molting is a natural process in which chickens lose and replace their feathers. It typically happens once a year in late fall, but depending on the breed, age, and environmental factors, the timing can vary. Molting can last anywhere from 3 to 19 weeks.

Molting can be stressful for chickens as it requires a lot of energy and resources from their bodies. During this time, hens may stop laying eggs or produce fewer eggs as their bodies redirect their resources toward growing new feathers. You may also notice that your chickens become more irritable or less active during molting.

To help your chickens through the molting process, it's important to provide them with a nutritious diet high in protein, such as mealworms, soldier fly larvae, black oil sunflower seeds, and scrambled eggs. You can also add supplements such as brewer's yeast or a commercial poultry supplement to their feed to support feather growth.

Feather Loss

Feather picking and cannibalism are also common problems in chickens, often caused by stress, overcrowding, or nutritional deficiencies. Feather picking can lead to feather loss and skin irritation, while cannibalism can result in serious injuries and even death. Chickens also tend to peck at wounds and sore spots on other hens, quickly making the problem much worse.

Preventative measures include providing adequate space, proper nutrition, and environmental enrichment, such as dust baths and perches. In cases of severe feather picking or cannibalism, it may be necessary to remove the more dominant or weaker hens from the flock.

Pasty Vent

Pasty vent, also known as vent gleet, is a common health problem in chickens that affects the area around the vent. It is caused by an overgrowth of yeast or bacteria and is often seen in young or stressed birds. The condition is characterized by a build-up of fecal matter around the vent, which can harden and cause irritation and inflammation.

A pasty vent can be treated by cleaning the affected area with warm water and gently removing the build-up of fecal matter. Keeping the area clean and dry is crucial to prevent the condition from recurring. In severe cases, antifungal or antibiotic medications may be necessary, and a veterinarian should be consulted for proper diagnosis and treatment.

PARASITIC DISEASES OF CHICKENS

Parasitic diseases are a common problem in chicken flocks, and they can significantly impact chicken health and productivity. As a chicken keeper, you will likely encounter a parasite problem at some point, and prompt recognition is the key to preventing this from becoming an infestation. Your first call for advice for any suspected parasitic infection should be to your local veterinary clinic.

External Parasites

External parasites include lice, mites, and fleas that feed on the chickens' blood and can cause skin irritation, feather loss, and anemia. Your hens will preen and take dust baths to keep external parasites under control, but in debilitated birds, they can quickly become a big problem.

Internal Parasites

Internal parasites such as roundworms, tapeworms, and coccidia can cause weight loss, diarrhea, and decreased egg production. Proper sanitation, regular deworming, and monitoring for signs of infestation can help prevent and manage these issues.

Protozoan Infections

Protozoan infections include diseases like histomoniasis, also known as "blackhead," which is caused by a protozoan that affects the liver and can cause significant mortality in chickens. This disease can be prevented by proper sanitation, avoiding overcrowding, and using preventative medication.

Fungal Infections

Fungal infections such as aspergillosis can cause respiratory distress. The risk of fungal infections can be prevented by maintaining proper ventilation and moisture levels in the chicken coop.

VIRAL AND BACTERIAL DISEASES OF CHICKENS

Viral and bacterial diseases are a major concern when it comes to the health and productivity of chicken flocks. These diseases can quickly spread, resulting in high mortality rates and reduced egg production. This can have a significant impact not only on the poultry industry but also on your backyard birds.

Proper biosecurity measures, vaccination, and treatment protocols are essential for managing and preventing the spread of these infectious diseases. If you suspect your chickens are suffering from a viral or bacterial disease, veterinary advice must be sought as soon as possible!

- Infectious bronchitis: A highly contagious respiratory disease that affects chickens of all ages. Symptoms include sneezing, coughing, nasal discharge, and decreased egg production.

- Marek's disease: A viral disease that affects the nervous system and immune systems of chickens. Symptoms include paralysis, weight loss, and tumors.

- Fowl pox: A viral disease that affects the skin and mucous membranes of chickens. Symptoms include wart-like lesions on the head, comb, and wattles.

- Newcastle disease: A highly contagious viral disease that affects the respiratory, nervous, and digestive systems of chickens. Symptoms include respiratory distress, nervous signs, and decreased egg production.

- Avian influenza: A highly contagious viral disease that can cause severe respiratory illness in chickens. It can spread rapidly and has the potential to cause significant mortality in poultry flocks.

- Avian tuberculosis: A chronic bacterial disease that affects multiple organs in chickens. Symptoms include weight loss, respiratory distress, and diarrhea.

- Infectious coryza: A bacterial disease that affects the respiratory system of chickens. Symptoms include nasal discharge, sneezing, and swelling around the eyes and face.

- Avian encephalomyelitis: A viral disease that affects the nervous system of chickens. Symptoms include tremors, loss of balance, and paralysis.

- Egg Drop Syndrome (EDS): A viral disease that affects the reproductive system of chickens, leading to decreased egg production and thin-shelled or misshapen eggs.

- Infectious Bursal Disease (Gumboro): A viral disease that affects the immune system of chickens, leading to immunosuppression and increased susceptibility to other diseases.

- Mycoplasmosis: A bacterial disease that affects the respiratory system of chickens. Symptoms include nasal discharge, coughing, and decreased egg production.

- Necrotic enteritis: A bacterial disease that affects the digestive system of chickens, leading to weight loss and mortality

- Salmonellosis: A bacterial disease that can cause enteritis and septicemia in chickens, leading to diarrhea and mortality.

POULTRY HEALTH ESSENTIALS – HOW TO PREVENT DISEASE IN YOUR FLOCK

Keeping your flock healthy is key to ensuring that your feathered friends are happy, productive, and laying delicious eggs. Fortunately, there are a few simple steps that you can take to help prevent disease in your flock and keep them in tip-top shape.

In this section, we'll share some essential poultry health tips that are both effective and easy to implement. From promoting good nutrition to practicing good hygiene, these tips will help you maintain a healthy and happy flock.

Nutrition: The Importance of a Balanced Diet for Healthy Hens

A balanced diet is essential for maintaining the health and productivity of your chickens. A lack of proper nutrition can lead to several health problems, including weakened immune systems, poor egg quality, and reduced laying rates. To ensure that your hens are getting the nutrition they need, provide a balanced diet that includes a variety of different foods. This can include commercial chicken feed, fresh fruits and vegetables, and supplements like calcium and grit. It's also vital to provide a continuous supply of clean, fresh water to keep your hens hydrated.

In addition to providing a balanced diet, it's important to monitor your hens' eating habits and adjust their diet as necessary. If you notice that your hens are losing weight, their feathers are looking dull, or their egg production has decreased, it may be a sign that they're not getting the nutrients they need. Consulting with a veterinarian or poultry nutritionist can help you develop a feeding plan that meets your hens' specific nutritional needs.

Hygiene: Maintaining a Clean and Sanitary Living Environment

Maintaining a clean and sanitary living environment is essential for preventing the spread of disease and keeping your chickens healthy. This includes regularly cleaning and disinfecting your coop and surrounding area, as well as providing clean bedding and nesting materials for your hens. It is also important to keep your flock's food and water sources clean and free of debris.

Regularly monitoring your chickens for signs of illness, such as coughing or sneezing, can help you detect and prevent the spread of disease early on. If you notice any signs of illness, it's important to isolate the affected bird and seek veterinary advice as soon as possible.

How to clean a chicken waterer and feeder

Regularly cleaning your chicken's waterers and feeders is essential to prevent the growth of harmful bacteria and other microorganisms. Start by emptying any remaining food or water from the containers, then scrub them with hot soapy water using a brush or sponge. Rinse thoroughly with clean water and allow to air dry completely before refilling. For an extra level of cleanliness, you can also use a pet-safe disinfectant solution and allow it to dry before refilling.

How to clean a chicken coop

Keeping your chicken coop clean is key to preventing disease and maintaining your hens' health. The coop and run should get a thorough cleaning two or three times per year, probably more often if you have a lot of chickens sharing the space. Start by removing all the bedding, including any manure, and dispose of it properly. Use a hose or pressure washer to thoroughly rinse the coop, paying special attention to any nooks and crannies where dirt and debris can accumulate. Once the coop is dry, you may want to use a poultry-safe disinfectant to kill any remaining bacteria or pathogens. Allow the disinfectant to dry completely before adding fresh bedding and allowing your hens back in. Remember to wear gloves and a mask while cleaning to protect yourself from any harmful bacteria or dust.

Biosecurity: Protecting Your Flock from Disease and Illness

Biosecurity measures are essential for protecting your flock from diseases and illnesses. This includes implementing measures to prevent the introduction of diseases onto your property, as well as taking steps to prevent the spread of disease within your flock.

To prevent the introduction of diseases, it's essential to practice good biosecurity measures such as quarantining new birds, limiting visitors to your property, and disinfecting equipment and vehicles that come into contact with your chickens. You should also refrain from purchasing birds from unknown or unreliable sources.

To prevent the spread of disease within your flock, you

should separate birds that are sick or showing signs of illness from the rest of the flock. Regularly cleaning and disinfecting your equipment and housing and implementing pest control measures can help prevent the spread of disease.

Preventative Care: Regular Health Checks, Parasite Control, and Vaccinations

Building a strong bond with your chickens from a young age by regularly handling them is crucial for making them more cooperative during health checks and care routines. Chicks learn to trust and perceive human touch as non-threatening when you gently interact with them. This trust naturally deepens over time, making tasks like health checks and administering medication much smoother and less stressful.

Observing your chickens and becoming familiar with their normal behavior and appearance is essential. Someone told us to check on the four F's: feet, feathers, features, and fatigue. Look out for changes in their behavior, like lethargy, decreased egg production, loss of appetite, or weight loss. Make sure none of your birds are injured or look disheveled. If you notice any changes in a chicken's behavior or appearance, you should separate the bird from the rest of the flock and consult a veterinarian for advice.

Give your feathered friends the best care possible by scheduling regular checkups, staying on top of parasite control, and ensuring they're up-to-date with their vaccinations. Regular checkups can help you detect and address health issues early on, while parasite control measures can help prevent the spread of diseases such as mites and lice. Vaccinations can also help protect your flock against common diseases such as Marek's disease and Newcastle disease.

Working with a veterinarian who specializes in poultry health can help you develop a preventative care plan that meets the specific needs of your flock. This may include regular physical exams, fecal testing for parasites, and regular vaccinations.

Behavioral Health: Keeping Your Hens Active, Stimulated, and Stress-Free

Just like humans, chickens can experience stress and anxiety, which can have a direct impact on their overall well-being and productivity. Providing your hens with a stimulating and stress-free environment can help promote good mental and physical health.

Environmental enrichment can be provided through various toys and activities, such as hanging treat balls and puzzle feeders. Many chickens enjoy perching and roosting, so providing them with branches and climbing bars can be fun and engaging for them.

Additionally, providing access to plenty of outdoor space can help keep your hens active and reduce stress. Encourage natural behaviors such as scratching, pecking, and dust-bathing, which can help keep their feathers and skin healthy. Provide plenty of fresh water and make sure the feed and water containers are regularly cleaned and refilled.

It is clear to see that keeping your hens healthy requires a multifaceted approach that includes proper nutrition, hygiene, biosecurity, preventative care, and attention to their behavioral health. By implementing these practices, you can help prevent disease and ensure a long, happy life for your feathered friends. Moreover, you can look forward to an ample supply of delectable eggs, ready to be savored by you and your family!

Common Chicken Ailments, Infections, Parasites, and
Injuries Table

SUMMARY

In this chapter, we've learned that chickens are amazing creatures, just like any other animal, they can get sick. From egg-laying disorders to pesky parasites and viral infections, we've covered a lot of ground regarding chicken health. But don't worry, keeping your hens healthy is easier than you might think!

Here are two important things to remember from this chapter: First, make sure to stay on top of keeping everything clean. Second, pay close attention to any changes in your chickens' behavior.

Remember, chicken health issues can worsen rapidly, so it's crucial to take action quickly if you notice any signs of illness in your flock. In the next chapter, we'll delve into natural remedies for pest control and chicken care to ensure the well-being of your flock. You might be surprised to find that you already have what you need in your pantry or growing in your herb garden! Many of these effective natural treatments and methods have stood the test of time and have been used for generations. We've done the legwork to gather these remedies to help you keep your chickens happy and healthy.

6

AT-HOME REMEDIES AND CARE
FOR COMMON CHICKEN
AILMENTS

*T*his bonus chapter shines a light on a variety of health challenges that your feathered friends might face. While commercial poultry farms might rely on veterinary services for every health hiccup, backyard chicken keepers can apply practical, at-home remedies and preventive measures. From the annoying peck of fowlpox to the itch of mites and the discomfort of respiratory infections, this chapter equips you with the knowledge to tackle common chicken health issues using remedies you can prepare in your kitchen or find in your garden. Embrace the wisdom of generations past and modern insights to ensure your chickens lead a healthy, happy life.

TACKLING FOWLPOX WITH AT-HOME SOLUTIONS

Fowlpox, a challenge as old as chicken keeping itself, presents in two forms: dry, appearing as scabs or wart-like lesions on unfeathered parts, and wet, impacting the respiratory tract. It primarily spreads through mosquitoes or direct contact with an infected bird. At the first sign of sickness, isolate the effected chicken to stem the tide of infection. Boosting the rest of the flock's immunity is critical. Enrich their diet with vitamins A, E, and selenium, which is found in leafy greens and whole grains, or through over-the-counter supplements.

For the dry lesions, gently applying aloe vera gel offers soothing relief and provides natural antiviral properties. To promote overall health, you can add apple cider vinegar to their water (a ratio of 1 tablespoon per gallon). Additionally aloe vera offers several benefits for chicken care. Applying aloe vera gel directly to the chicken's skin can help with skin and feather health. For treating minor cuts and abrasions, gently applying aloe vera gel to the affected area can promote faster healing due to its antimicrobial properties. To aid their digestion and boost overall health, add a small amount of aloe vera juice to their drinking water (about four table-spoons per gallon). A 2022 study published by the U.S. National Institutes of Health has shown this method also has a calming effect on stressed chickens and encourages weight gain in broiler chicks. For a natural coop cleaner, you can mix aloe vera juice with water to create a safe, natural disin-fectant. It's amazingly versatile!

You can also mitigate mosquitoes by draining standing water. Not only will your chickens have a better chance of avoiding fowlpox, but your family and neighbors will prob-ably be happy, too.

COMBATTING MITES

Mites can pose another problem for your chickens. By care-fully observing your birds' behavior and condition, you can identify their presence early and prevent a full-blown siege.

Diatomaceous earth, a fine powder made from the fossilized remains of ancient algae, is a natural first line of defense. Spread in nesting spots and dust bathing areas, it works as a physical deterrent to these tiny pests. A mixture of garlic and apple cider vinegar, a teaspoon of each per liter of water, is another natural deterrent, making your chickens less appetizing to pests. Spraying diluted neem oil, a natural pesticide available at home and garden stores, within the coop lays down an invisible barrier against mites.

To further guard against mite infestation, alongside regular coop cleanings consider making a spray using essential oils known for their pest-repellent properties. Here's how:

Ingredients:

- **One spray bottle:** we use the 32 oz size so there is enough headroom in the bottle to effectively shake the mixture.
- **Base**: Use 16 ounces of distilled water as the base.
- **Dispersing Agent**: Add 4 ounces of witch hazel or alcohol to help mix the essential oils with water, ensuring the solution is gentle enough for chickens.
- **Essential Oils**: Use only 5-6 drops of essential oils per 20 ounces of liquid. This minimizes the risk of irritation or adverse reactions.
- **Lavender Oil**: 2 drops for its calming effect and pleasant scent.
- **Peppermint Oil**: 2 drops for its strong, pest-repelling scent.
- **Eucalyptus Oil**: 1 drop for its additional repellent qualities and fresh aroma.

- **Tea Tree or Lemongrass Oil**: Choose 1 drop of either tea tree oil for its potent antimicrobial properties or lemongrass oil for its insect-repellent properties, depending on your preference or based on what you observe to be more effective or tolerated by your chickens.

Application and Precautions:

- **Application**: Spray the mixture around the perimeter of the coop, focusing on the corners, edges, and any possible entry points for pests. Also spray the roosting areas and nesting boxes where your chickens will be spending their time. A general rule of thumb is to shake the spray bottle occasionally to keep it mixed and spray until these areas are damp but not soaking wet. This usually amounts to a few spritzes per square yard, ensuring the coop is well-coated but not drenched. It's best to do this at a time when the chickens can be safely removed from the coop to avoid direct contact with the spray, allowing the treated areas to air out for a bit before letting the chickens back in.
- **Frequency**: Apply the diluted spray every other week to maintain a deterrent against pests without overwhelming your chickens with strong scents.
- **Safety First**: Always observe your chickens for any signs of distress or discomfort after using the spray, and discontinue use immediately if any adverse effects are noted.

This spray offers a safe and effective way to maintain a

healthy coop, combining the benefits of essential oils with natural safety measures.

LICE AND EXTERNAL PARASITES: NATURE'S OWN PEST CONTROL

If you find lice on your chickens, enhance their dust baths and the coop's bedding with fine sand, wood ash, and diatomaceous earth. These additions give chickens a natural way to eliminate the pests themselves. Also, start applying the essential oil spray you've made for mite prevention—it's just as effective against lice. Make it a routine to inspect your flock regularly for any signs of lice or other external parasites. Early detection and immediate action are key to keeping your chickens healthy and happy. This approach combines the natural pest-fighting benefits of essential oils with straightforward, preventive care practices.

REMEDIES FOR RESPIRATORY INFECTIONS

When you hear signs of breathing troubles in your chickens, it's time to step in with some easy fixes. Echinacea and oregano, known for their antimicrobial properties, can be mixed into their feed or water. These herbs can be grown in your garden or found in your pantry and support your chickens' respiratory systems. Ensure the air in your coop stays fresh by keeping it well-ventilated but not so open that there are cold drafts. Also, try not to crowd too many chickens into a tiny coop. Mix some garlic or turmeric into some warm food for a healthy boost when they seem a bit off. These kitchen spices can help them feel better and strengthen their immune system.

COCCIDIOSIS

Keeping the coop clean and not too crowded is the key to preventing coccidiosis, a disease caused by a tiny parasite. Make sure to clean the coop regularly and keep the bedding dry to lower the risk of this parasite spreading. Also, when you get new chickens, it's a good idea to keep them separate from your main flock for about 14 to 21 days. This quarantine time lets you watch for any signs of sickness, like diarrhea or being unusually tired, and make sure they're healthy before they join the others.

Once you've done these preventive steps, there are a couple more things to keep your chickens healthy. Try adding apple cider vinegar to their drinking water (about 1 tablespoon per gallon), which acts as a gentle antiparasitic and helps with digestion. Feeding them probiotic-rich foods, such as fermented feed or a bit of natural yogurt, can also help keep their gut health in check, protecting them from infections.

AVIAN INFLUENZA:

For backyard chicken keepers, safeguarding your flock against avian influenza starts at home. Ensuring your chickens have secure housing minimizes their contact with wild birds, which is a critical step in preventing the spread of the virus. Quarantine any birds you suspect of having this virus immediately. Avian influenza is highly infectious, and suspected cases should be reported immediately to your local animal health authorities. It can have severe consequences on both birds and humans.

Cooperation with local agricultural authorities and the prompt reporting of bird flu contribute to the greater good, informing other poultry keepers across the region of the threat so they can protect their birds and hopefully stop it from spreading.

The symptoms of avian influenza in birds can vary from mild to severe, depending on the strain of the virus. Here are some common symptoms observed in birds:

Mild Symptoms

- Ruffled feathers
- Reduced egg production or soft-shelled or misshapen eggs
- Minor respiratory issues

Severe Symptoms

- Sudden death without any visible symptoms
- Swelling of the head, eyelids, comb, wattles, and hocks
- Purple discoloration of the wattles, combs, and legs
- Nasal discharge
- Coughing and sneezing
- Incoordination
- Diarrhea

CONCLUSION

At-home chicken care mixes traditional wisdom with modern insights, framing a holistic approach to nurturing our backyard flocks. By adopting the at-home remedies and preventive strategies detailed in this chapter, chicken keepers not only address the immediate health concerns of their feathered friends but also create an environment where these birds can flourish.

In the next chapter, get ready to dive into the entertaining and fascinating world of chicken behavior and how they communicate and interact with each other. Did you know that chickens have their own unique personalities and social hierarchies? We'll explore all of that and more, so get ready for some clucking good fun!

7

THE PECKING ORDER

*I*n this chapter, we will embark on a fascinating journey into the world of chicken behavior. By delving into the intricacies of their actions, instincts, and social dynamics, we will come to understand the fascinating world that these remarkable creatures live in.

However, you may wonder why learning about chicken behavior is so important as a backyard chicken keeper? Well, understanding chicken behavior is not only important for the well-being of your flock. It can also give you a more rewarding and enriching experience as a backyard chicken keeper. When we first started raising hens, we did so for the same reasons as many people – to get a source of fresh eggs for our family. However, over time we came to appreciate how fascinating these feathered creatures really are!

By unraveling the mysteries of chicken behavior, you gain valuable insights into their needs, preferences, and overall welfare. Recognizing their natural instincts and behaviors allows you to create an environment that caters to their physical and psychological well-being. From providing appropriate housing and nutrition to ensuring social harmony within the flock, understanding their behavior helps you become a responsible and attentive chicken keeper.

Although chickens are often perceived as unintelligent, they actually have distinct personalities and a proper social structure. You can forge a stronger bond with your feathered friends by comprehending their behavior. Recognizing their individual quirks, preferences, and communication signals allows you to better understand their emotions and needs. This connection fosters mutual trust and respect, making the experience of raising chickens all the more rewarding.

When you study chicken behavior, you will also learn to identify patterns, social dynamics, and stressors that may indicate a problem with your hens. This will help you promptly address issues and ensure your flock remains harmonious and peaceful.

On a personal level, many people find that observing chicken behavior provides a fascinating glimpse into the remarkable intricacies of the natural world. Witnessing their instinctive foraging, social hierarchies, and protective behaviors offers a window into the evolutionary adaptations that have shaped these birds over millennia. Observing their communication through vocalizations, body language, and displays is a fascinating study of nonverbal communication and the diversity of life on our planet.

As a chicken keeper, exploring chicken behavior is a continuous journey of learning and discovery. As you delve into the depths of their actions, you will learn about ethology, animal psychology, and the interconnectedness of living organisms. This understanding not only enriches your experience as a chicken keeper but also broadens your appreciation for the wonders of the natural world.

So, without any further ado, let us embark on this

exciting journey together and uncover the secret lives of our feathered companions!

CHICKEN COOP HIERARCHY: THE PECKING ORDER

To understand chicken behavior, we first need to explore the pecking order concept—the cornerstone of chicken social dynamics. The term "pecking order" refers to the established hierarchy within a flock, where each chicken occupies a specific rank or position based on dominance and submission.

Just as humans have social structures and hierarchies, chickens also have a complex system that governs their interactions and relationships. The pecking order determines the flock's social order, influence, and access to resources. It is a means for chickens to establish and maintain stability, reduce aggression, and promote cooperative behavior.

The phrase "pecking order" stems from the behavior of chickens pecking at each other as a form of communication and assertion of dominance. However, this social hierarchy encompasses more than just pecking; it includes a range of behaviors such as body language, vocalizations, wing displays, and even subtle posturing.

By recognizing these dynamics within the flock, you can take steps to prevent excessive aggression and create a harmonious living environment for your chickens. Moreover, knowing the pecking order of your flock enables you to identify potential stressors, ensure fair access to resources like food and water, and minimize the risk of injury or social exclusion.

Purpose of the Pecking Order

The pecking order serves a vital purpose within a chicken flock. It establishes a structured social hierarchy that helps maintain order, minimize aggression, and ensure the efficient allocation of resources. By having a clear pecking order, chickens can establish their place in the social hierarchy, reducing the need for constant confrontations and potential injuries.

Within the pecking order, each chicken has a designated rank or position. The highest-ranking individual, often referred to as the "alpha" or "dominant" bird, holds the most influence and privileges. Other chickens occupy progressively lower positions in the hierarchy, with the lowest-ranking individuals often experiencing social challenges and limited access to resources.

Understanding the purpose of the pecking order allows chicken keepers to recognize that social hierarchies are a natural part of a flock's social structure. While it may involve occasional conflicts, it helps maintain stability, establish social norms, and ensure the overall well-being of the flock.

Chicken Hierarchy Explained

Chickens establish a hierarchy wherever they gather, including the coop, the run, and even during free-ranging activities. The dynamics of this pecking order can vary widely, depending on the type and number of chickens present in the flock, and even a small group of two or three hens can have a complex social structure.

To understand the intricacies of the chicken coop hierarchy, we need to look at the key players:

The Rooster

Although it would be easy to assume that the rooster is at

the top of the pecking order, this is not necessarily the case. Hens and roosters have separate pecking orders, but the most dominant birds of each gender will work together for the overall benefit of the flock.

When a single rooster lives with a group of hens, he takes on the role of leader and protector. He keeps a watchful eye on the flock, alerting them to potential threats. He also guides the hens during foraging activities and finds the very best morsels of food to share with them. A rooster clucking to call his hens when he's found something particularly tasty to eat truly is an adorable sound to hear!

The ultimate aim of a rooster is to reproduce, so you may see them performing courtship displays, such as wing dragging, dancing, and vocalizations, to attract and mate with the hens. They also play a role in maintaining the harmony of the flock by intervening in disputes and breaking up aggressive encounters between hens.

Most backyard chicken keepers only keep one rooster, but if you have two or more males, the social dynamics can become very interesting indeed! Each rooster will aim to secure his own flock, preferably with the very best hens of his choosing. To do this, roosters will establish a hierarchy to determine the social standing of each male. The highest-ranking rooster tends to have preferential access to food, water, and mating opportunities.

Dominant roosters typically exhibit assertive behaviors, such as strutting, crowing, wing displays, and vocalizations, to establish their authority over subordinate roosters. This helps to minimize physical confrontations and maintain social order. While conflicts may occasionally arise, roosters often engage in ritualized displays and posturing rather than engaging in outright aggression.

If you keep more than one rooster, you will need enough hens to let them both have their own small flock. Hens may switch between flocks, but each rooster will most likely have one or two favorite hens that stick by his side. If one rooster appears to be isolated without any company, it may be time to find him a new home with hens of his own.

The Dominant Hen

The dominant hen holds the highest position in the pecking order and enjoys certain privileges and resources within the flock. She also plays a crucial role in shaping the social dynamics and maintaining order among the hens. She typically has priority access to food, water, preferred nesting boxes, and roosting spots.

The dominant hen will establish her authority through a combination of assertive behaviors, body language, and vocalizations. Her confidence will set the tone for the rest of the flock, and other hens typically show respect and submission towards her. She may also chase or peck lower-ranking individuals to reinforce her dominance, particularly when new or younger hens join the flock.

Dominant hens tend to be bolder and more outgoing and will often assume the role of a rooster in a hen-only flock by leading the other hens on foraging expeditions. However, unlike a rooster, a dominant hen will keep all the best food for herself!

When a rooster is present, the most dominant hens may receive more attention and protection from him, as they hold higher social status and are likely to produce offspring with desirable genetic traits.

The Rest Of The Flock

Although the rooster and the dominant hen are the key players in our chicken hierarchy, that doesn't mean the rest of the hens hang around in a friendly gang! The social scale continues downwards, with each hen jostling to be as high in the pecking order as possible. Over time an established flock will live happily together with minimal conflict, but if you watch closely, you will see that the dominant birds quite literally rule the roost!

HOW FLOCK MANAGEMENT AND COOP DESIGN AFFECTS THE PECKING ORDER

The way you manage your flock and design their coop can have a big influence on the pecking order and the dynamics among your chickens. It's important to consider factors like available space, how resources are distributed, and introducing new chickens into the mix. These elements all play a role in shaping the relationships within your feathered crew.

A cramped or overcrowded coop can intensify social tensions and lead to more frequent aggressive behaviors. A key area of conflict is on the roosting bars, as each hen jostles for a premium position to settle down for the night. A chicken run that is too small also frequently leads to bullying, as the less dominant hens are unable to escape and hide.

Providing ample space both inside the coop and in the run allows chickens to establish their territories and minimize competition for resources. For larger flocks of hens, provide food and water in two or more locations to ensure all hens have equal access.

Introducing new chickens to an existing flock can temporarily disrupt the pecking order. During the integration process, chickens may engage in squabbles and posturing as they establish their new ranks. Careful monitoring and gradual introductions, such as through a wire barrier or supervised free-ranging, can help minimize conflicts and promote a smoother integration.

MITIGATING TERRITORIAL DISPUTES

Territorial disputes are common within a chicken flock and can result from establishing or reshuffling the pecking order. As new chickens mature or flock dynamics change, conflicts may arise as individuals assert their dominance. To some extent, you may need to let nature take its course here, but it pays to be vigilant and intervene when necessary to reduce the risk of bullying and injuries.

To mitigate territorial disputes, chicken keepers can employ several strategies. Providing multiple feeding and watering stations reduces competition and allows lower-ranking chickens to access essential resources without interference. Incorporating environmental enrichment, such as perches, hiding spots, and distractions like hanging treats, can divert attention and reduce aggression.

If conflicts persist, separating aggressive individuals temporarily or using visual barriers to create subdivisions within the coop can help calm tensions. Gradual reintroduction and supervision during reintegration can allow chickens to readjust their positions in the pecking order without excessive aggression.

NORMAL CHICKEN BEHAVIOR

As well as understanding the behavioral dynamics of your chicken flock, it also pays to learn about chicken behavior on an individual level. Even after just a few days of keeping chickens, you will come to realize that each bird has its own personality traits, and they all display some fascinating behaviors.

Let's take a look at some of the behaviors you will likely observe within your flock:

- Individual Recognition: Chickens possess the ability to recognize and distinguish between individuals within their flock. Through visual cues, vocalizations, and familiarity with each other's unique characteristics, chickens can identify their flock mates. This recognition enables them to establish social bonds, form alliances, and navigate the social interactions within the flock.

- Preening: Preening is a vital grooming behavior for chickens. Using their beaks, they carefully clean and arrange their feathers, removing dirt, parasites, and excess oils. Preening helps maintain feather health, insulation, and overall cleanliness. Additionally, preening serves as a social behavior, with chickens often preening each other as a form of bonding and establishing social connections.

- Fighting: Although less common in well-managed flocks, fighting among chickens may occur as your birds establish a pecking order or settle territorial disputes. Although physical contact is uncommon, aggressive encounters such as pecking, wing flapping, charging, and vocalizations often occur. While some level of aggression is natural, excessive fighting or bullying can be detrimental to flock harmony and should be monitored and addressed promptly.

- Foraging: Foraging is a deeply-rooted instinctive behavior in chickens. They actively explore their environment in search of food, pecking and scratching the ground to uncover insects, seeds, plants, and other edible items. Letting your chickens forage not only gives them vital nutrition but also offers a way for them to stay active and engaged. It allows them to express their natural behaviors and follow their instincts. This promotes their overall physical and mental well-being.

- Nesting: Nesting behavior is crucial for egg-laying hens. Before laying an egg, hens will seek out secluded and comfortable spots, scratching and arranging nesting materials to their satisfaction. Nesting serves as a protective and comfortable environment for the hens to lay their eggs, ensuring the safety and successful incubation of their offspring.

- Dust Bathing: Don't overlook the importance of dust bathing for chickens! It's a crucial behavior that helps them keep their feathers and skin in tip-top condition. By engaging in dust bathing, they maintain their overall feather and skin health. Chickens use their beaks and feet to create shallow depressions in loose soil or dust and then vigorously flap and roll around in it. This helps to remove excess oils, parasites, and dead skin from their feathers and skin while also providing a means of thermoregulation and relaxation.

- Perching: Chickens have a natural instinct to perch, as they prefer elevated surfaces for roosting and resting. This behavior helps them feel secure, have a better view of their surroundings, and stay away from potential ground-based dangers. By offering suitable perching options in the coop, you promote these natural behaviors, support their physical well-being, and encourage restful sleep.

- Responding To Fluctuating Temperatures: When the weather is too warm for comfort, your hens will seek shade to cool down. They will also exhibit behaviors such as spreading their wings to increase airflow, panting to regulate body temperature, and reducing activity levels during the hottest parts of the day. Adequate access to shade, ventilation, and freshwater is essential to help chickens maintain their comfort and prevent heat stress during hot weather. Conversely, chickens will also alter their behavior during cold or wet weather. They will huddle together for warmth, especially when roosting at night, and reduce their activity levels to conserve energy.

- Drinking: Ensuring chickens have regular access to clean and fresh water is crucial for their overall health and well-being. They use their beaks to sip and swallow water, and they will adjust their intake as needed, especially in hot weather or when consuming dry feed. It's worth noting that chickens generally prefer cold water over sun-warmed water, so it's important to provide fresh, cool water daily to meet their hydration needs. Many chicken owners, ourselves included, have observed this behavior in our birds.

- Social Learning: Chickens are capable of learning new social skills by observing and imitating the behaviors of other flock members. They can acquire new foraging techniques and problem-solving skills and adapt to changes in their environment. Social learning plays a significant role in transmitting knowledge and behaviors within the flock, contributing to their collective adaptability and survival.

- Communication: Chickens communicate through a variety of vocalizations, body language, and visual signals. Each vocalization serves a different purpose, enabling your hens to express contentment, alert others to danger, or assert dominance. Body language, such as wing displays, head movements, and posture, also conveys important messages within the flock.

Here are some of the most common noises you will hear from your flock and what they mean:

- Clucking: Chickens often cluck softly while foraging or exploring their surroundings. This can indicate contentment and a sense of calm within the flock. It is a reassuring sound that signifies everything is normal and peaceful.

- Cackling: When a hen lays an egg, she may produce a distinctive cackling sound. This serves as an announcement to the flock, alerting them to the accomplishment and sometimes attracting attention from other hens.

- Squawking: Squawking is a loud and often harsh vocalization that chickens use to indicate distress, fear, or agitation. It may occur when a chicken feels threatened by a predator or when facing a potentially dangerous situation. Squawking is also a way for chickens to communicate warnings to the rest of the flock about potential dangers.

- Crowing: Roosters are known for their crowing, which is a series of loud and distinct calls. Crowing is a way for roosters to establish their territory, assert dominance, and communicate their presence to other roosters and the flock. The crowing can also serve as a morning wake-up call and announce their presence to potential mates.

- Purring: Ever heard of chickens purring? Just like a cat's purr, some chickens emit a low and vibrating sound when they're content and relaxed. It's their way of expressing happiness during positive social interactions, like when they're enjoying some friendly pets.

- Chirping: Chirping is a common sound made by chicks. It is a high-pitched, repetitive noise that signifies their well-being and contentment. Chirping also serves as a way for chicks to communicate with their mother hen and siblings, maintaining contact and ensuring their safety within the brood.

CHICK BEHAVIOR

To finish this chapter on the social world of chickens, we are going to take a quick look at the captivating world of chick behavior and how they interact with their mothers.

When hens successfully hatch chicks, their remarkable maternal instincts kick in, and it's pretty amazing to see.

They provide warmth, protection, and guidance to their little ones. They reassure and guide the chicks with soft clucking sounds while giving them warm and safe shelter under their wings. The presence of the hen creates a sense of security and teaches the chicks essential life skills like foraging, dust bathing, and socializing. It's a beautiful display of nature's wonders right in your backyard!

As chicks grow and gain confidence, they begin to explore a variety of behaviors when interacting with their peers. This is a crucial phase for their social development. You'll often see them engage in playful activities like chasing, pecking, and exploring together. These interactions are how they learn vital social skills, figure out their place in the pecking order, and form relationships that will influence their behavior as they mature. It's a fascinating process to witness!

SUMMARY

It is clear to see that understanding chicken behavior is a fundamental aspect of raising backyard chickens. By delving into the social dynamics within the flock, exploring individual behaviors, and recognizing the unique relationships between hens, roosters, and chicks, we can create an environment that promotes their well-being, natural instincts, and overall happiness. Through careful flock management, coop design, and providing adequate resources, we can help establish a harmonious pecking order, foster positive social interactions, and support the development of a thriving flock.

In the next chapter we will delve into the factors influencing egg production, how to ensure egg quality and safety, as well as valuable tips for marketing and selling eggs. Whether you're a backyard chicken enthusiast or an aspiring egg entrepreneur, the next chapter will provide invaluable insights into the world of egg production and its potential benefits. So sit back, relax, and let's crack open the egg-citing adventure ahead!

8

EGGS IN YOUR BASKET

*E*ggs have experienced a remarkable surge in popularity in recent years. With a growing number of families choosing to consume eggs as a delicious and nutritious protein source, the demand for these versatile oval wonders has soared, and so has the price. It is now thought that the average person consumes roughly the same number of eggs as a single hen will lay in a year.

This burgeoning appetite for eggs has had a notable impact on the market. According to the Consumer Price Index data, egg prices in December witnessed a staggering 60% increase in 2022 compared to the previous year. This reflects the growing demand for eggs and their increasing value as a staple food item.

As poultry keepers, it's essential to understand the dynamics of egg production and learn how to sell them effectively to make the most out of their flock. This includes a knowledge of the various factors influencing egg quantity, quality, and consistency. A successful egg-production business also requires the knowledge and strategies to navigate the market confidently.

Within this chapter, we are going to delve into the secrets of successful egg production and reveal the keys to unlocking the market's potential. We will explore the fascinating world of eggs, from the moment they are laid to the gratifying experience of sharing the fruits of your labor with eager customers. So, gather your curiosity and prepare to embark on a chapter dedicated to the wonders of egg production and the art of selling!

EGG PRODUCTION

So, you've got your new hens happily settled in their coop, and now is the time to reap the rewards of all the time and money you've invested in your flock so far! There is nothing quite like the excitement of finding a clutch of eggs in the nesting box, most likely accompanied by the proud squawking of a hen that has laid her first-ever egg!

As a backyard chicken keeper, your main goal is most likely to have a flock of healthy, happy hens that provide you with a regular supply of eggs. In the previous chapters, we have covered everything you need to do to maximize the egg-laying potential of your hens, from providing suitable accommodations and nutrition to managing health problems in your flock.

How Often Do Chickens Lay Eggs?

One of the fascinating aspects of raising chickens is observing their remarkable ability to produce eggs. However, egg-laying frequency can vary depending on several factors, including breed, age, health, and environmental conditions. Understanding these factors is the key to ensuring optimal egg production from your flock.

Chickens typically start laying eggs when they reach

maturity, which is usually around 5 to 6 months of age. However, this timeline can vary slightly between breeds and depends on the time of year the hen was born. Egg-laying is triggered by lengthening daylight hours in the spring, and a young hen will not start to lay until there are at least 14 hours between sunrise and sunset.

Once they begin laying, most hens follow a predictable pattern of egg production. Generally, a healthy hen will lay an egg every 24 to 26 hours, with some variations depending on the individual bird.

In an ideal world, every hen would lay an egg every day, but it doesn't always work like this! Levels of egg production vary widely between breeds, but even the most prolific egg layers may skip a day every week or so. As a rule of thumb, it is a good idea to expect each hen to lay four or five eggs a week – any more than this should be considered a bonus!

It is important to note that egg production can be influenced by various factors, such as the amount and quality of feed provided, the presence of adequate lighting, and seasonal changes. Some hybrid chicken breeds will lay eggs nearly year-round, whereas more traditional breeds will take a break during the winter months. Most chicken keepers also notice a drop in egg production during the annual feather molting period.

Additionally, as your chickens grow older, their egg production may decrease gradually. This is a natural part of the aging process, but how rapidly it occurs varies amongst individual hens. In a backyard flock, it can be hard to spot which hens are not laying as frequently, so a hen that is no longer laying can often go unnoticed.

By understanding the typical egg-laying patterns of your specific chicken breed and providing them with optimal care, nutrition, and suitable environmental conditions, you can help ensure consistent and satisfactory egg production from your flock.

When to Collect Eggs

This might sound like a simple topic, but there is more to collecting eggs than you might expect! In an established flock, it is just a matter of going into the coop at regular times to collect the eggs, but younger point-of-lay hens rely on other egg-laying hens to guide them to the best places to lay.

In the chicken hierarchy, the dominant hen normally lays first, and she will select the best nesting box to do this. The remainder of the flock will wait to use this box, which is why you often find all the eggs crowded into one nest! A larger flock may use two or more nesting boxes, but you will still find that they favor one more than all the rest.

So, when your young hens start laying, they rely on an older hen to pave the way and show them the best nesting box to use. If your junior hens keep laying their eggs in undesirable places, such as in the run, pop some eggs into the nesting box to guide them. Leaving a few eggs in the nesting box gives these young hens a helpful hint about where they should lay their own eggs. It's all about providing them with a bit of guidance and setting them up for success.

The timing of egg collection also plays a vital role in maintaining egg quality and freshness. Collecting eggs promptly after they are laid helps to prevent them from deteriorating or becoming contaminated – they should never be left in the coop for longer than necessary. Daily collection minimizes the chances of eggs becoming soiled, broken, or pecked by other chickens.

Delayed collection of eggs can lead to the absorption of bacteria through the porous shell, increasing the risk of spoilage and reducing the shelf life of the eggs. During extremely hot or cold weather, it may be necessary to collect eggs more frequently to prevent them from overheating or freezing.

How to Collect Eggs

Once your flock is consistently laying in the right place, it is time to get into an egg-collecting routine. Set a specific time each day to collect eggs to help prevent them from piling up. This will reduce the risk of breakage or accidental trampling. Most hens lay in the morning, so we tend to collect our eggs at lunchtime. If a hen is still sitting when you enter the coop, leave her in peace to finish laying and come back for the eggs later.

Before you dive in and pick up the eggs, take a quick peek at them – any that are broken or look abnormal should be carefully removed to avoid contaminating the rest of the batch. As you pick up the eggs from the nesting box, handle them carefully to avoid cracking or damaging the shells. Hold them gently, supporting the entire egg with your hand to distribute pressure evenly.

A rookie mistake that many people make is to overestimate how many eggs they can carry! It is always so disappointing when you drop an egg, so use a basket or container to carry them. Before you leave the coop with your basket of eggs, make sure the nesting boxes are clean and tidy, removing any soiled bedding and replacing it with fresh, clean material.

Cleaning and Storing Eggs

Ensuring proper cleanliness and storage practices are vital for preserving the quality and safety of your eggs. Fresh eggs have a natural protective coating called the bloom or cuticle, which acts as a barrier against bacteria entering the shell. Excessive washing can strip away this protective layer, making the eggs more susceptible to contamination. Therefore, it is recommended to only wash eggs with visible dirt or stains. When you do have to clean an egg, here is some advice for you:

Start by gently removing any visible dirt or debris from the eggshell using a soft brush or cloth. Avoid using abrasive materials that can damage the cuticle or shell. If stubborn stains or dirt can't be easily removed, you can lightly dampen a cloth or sponge with warm water (approximately 90°F.) Make sure the water is slightly warmer than the temperature of the egg. Gently wipe the dirty areas of the eggshell with a damp cloth or sponge. Avoid scrubbing too hard because that can damage the cuticle. If necessary, you can use a mild, food-grade sanitizing solution specifically designed for egg cleaning, but use it sparingly! Follow the instructions on the product carefully and be gentle. When finished, rinse the eggshell with clean water to remove any residue. Pat it dry with a clean, lint-free cloth or paper towel. Avoid using heat to dry your eggs because that can affect the egg's quality.

One great advantage of eggs is their impressively long shelf life – if stored correctly, they can last for over a month. Place eggs in an egg tray or box with the smaller pointed end facing downwards. This position helps preserve the quality and integrity of the eggs over time. Use a pencil, permanent marker, or, if you want to get fancy, a purpose-made egg stamp to mark each egg with the date it was laid.

When it comes to selling the eggs your chickens lay, it is generally recommended to wash and refrigerate them to comply with health codes and regulations. However, eating unwashed and unrefrigerated eggs is considered safe for personal use as long as they are fresh. Remember, it's always a good idea to check with local authorities and follow your area's specific food safety guidelines to ensure you meet the necessary safety and quality standards. Better safe than sorry, right?

Testing Egg Freshness

If you are in any doubt about how fresh your eggs are, try one of these simple tests to check they are okay to consume:

- The Float Test: Fill a bowl with water and gently place the egg in it. Fresh eggs will sink and lay flat on the bottom. Eggs that are not as fresh but still safe to consume will stand upright on the bottom. If the egg floats or stands on end, it is no longer fresh and should be discarded.

- The Shake Test: Hold the egg close to your ear and shake it gently. Fresh eggs will produce minimal sound or remain silent. If you hear a sloshing sound, it may indicate that the egg's contents have deteriorated, indicating reduced freshness.

- Visual Examination: Cracked or broken shells, moldy or off-putting odors, or discolored or excessively runny egg whites are signs that an egg is not fresh and should be discarded.

WHY ARE MY CHICKENS EATING THEIR EGGS?

Discovering that your chickens are eating their eggs can be disheartening and frustrating. However, understanding the possible reasons behind egg eating is crucial for addressing the issue. Here are some common reasons why chickens may develop this unfortunate habit:

- Nutritional deficiencies: Chickens might consume their eggs if their diet lacks essential nutrients, particularly calcium. Ensure your flock's feed contains the necessary vitamins and minerals to meet their nutritional requirements.

- Broken or weak shells: If eggs are easily broken due to thin or weak shells, chickens may accidentally peck or crack them, leading to a taste for eggs. Provide a calcium supplement or oyster shells to strengthen the shells and prevent breakages.

- Boredom or stress: Chickens might eat eggs if they are bored, stressed, or lack proper stimulation. Ensure they have enough space, perches, toys, and opportunities for foraging to keep them mentally and physically stimulated.

- Poor nest box conditions: Dirty or cramped nest boxes may encourage hens to peck at and eat their eggs. Maintain clean and comfortable nesting areas to discourage this behavior.

- Learned behavior: Chickens may observe other birds pecking or eating eggs and mimic this behavior. Address the issue promptly to prevent it from spreading within the flock.

To deter egg eating, ensure that your hens have a well-balanced diet, maintain clean and spacious nesting areas, and provide adequate mental and physical stimulation for your chickens. Collect eggs regularly to remove temptation, and consider placing 'fake' eggs like golf balls in the nesting box to break the habit.

HOW TO HATCH CHICKEN EGGS

If you are considering breeding new egg-layers or meat chickens to add to your flock, you will need to learn how to hatch chicken eggs. Hatching chicken eggs can be an immensely rewarding experience, allowing you to witness the miracle of life unfold before your eyes. It is also a very cost-effective way to expand your flock, particularly if you have a broody hen to do the work for you!

However, waiting for a hen to go broody isn't always practical, particularly if your chosen breed of hen does not have strong mothering instincts. If you want to hatch eggs on a regular basis, most chicken owners opt to use an incubator instead.

When embarking on the journey of incubating and hatching chicken eggs, there are several key points to bear in mind:

- Ensure that the eggs you intend to hatch are fertile. This requires having a rooster in the flock for mating with the hens. If you don't have a rooster or want specific chicken breeds, you can easily find fertile eggs for sale, allowing you to hatch your own chicks to expand your flock.

- Invest in a reliable egg incubator that provides consistent temperature and humidity control, and follow the manufacturer's instructions for optimal usage. For most incubators, the optimum conditions are 100.5 degrees Fahrenheit with 50-55 percent humidity.

- Select eggs of good quality and size, free from cracks or deformities. Fresh eggs that are just a day or two old have higher hatching rates.

- Eggs should be regularly turned during incubation to prevent the embryo from sticking to the shell and facilitate even development. If your incubator does not have an egg-turning function, you will need to turn them by hand five times a day.

- On the tenth day of incubation, you can use a process called candling to observe the development and viability of the embryo. This process helps identify and remove any non-viable or spoiled eggs. We recommend watching a video of this technique online. **There will be a QR link to one at the end of the chapter!**

- The hatching process should start around 21 days after setting your eggs in the incubator. During this period, maintain stable conditions in the incubator and resist the urge to interfere; it is vital to remain patient and allow nature to take its course.

- Once the chicks hatch, they require a warm and protected environment, ideally in a purpose-made brooder box. This should be prepared with appropriate heat sources, bedding, feed, and water to ensure the well-being of your newly-hatched chicks.

Do Chickens Ever Stop Laying Eggs?

While chickens are renowned for their egg-laying abilities, their productivity is not indefinite. As hens age, their egg production tends to decline. Generally, hens reach peak egg production in their first year and gradually lay fewer eggs as they get older. By the time they reach 3 to 4 years of age, egg production may significantly decrease. There are definitely exceptions to this; a friend of ours has two hens who are about 10 years old that still lay pretty regularly.

Different chicken breeds have varying egg-laying capabilities. Some breeds are known for their high egg production throughout their lifespan, while others may have shorter egg-laying spans. Hybrid egg-laying hens often produce eggs daily for around a year, after which production slows down considerably. Traditional chicken breeds produce fewer eggs per week but continue to lay regularly for several years.

Egg production can also fluctuate with seasonal changes. During the colder months and shorter daylight periods, hens may enter a period of reduced egg production or even cease laying altogether. This is a natural response to changes in daylight and environmental conditions. During the molting period, in late summer or early fall, hens may temporarily cease egg production.

WHAT TO DO WITH HENS THAT HAVE STOPPED LAYING EGGS

But eventually, regardless of seasonal changes, you will reach a point when older hens stop laying altogether. As a backyard chicken owner, it can sometimes be challenging to determine which hens are no longer laying eggs and what to do with them.

It is important to note that even if hens stop laying eggs,

they may still have value as beloved pets or for their contribution to the overall well-being of the flock. Many chicken owners – ourselves included – are happy to let our elderly hens live out their retirement years with the rest of the flock. After all, they've earned it with the number of eggs they have produced for us over their lifetime!

Hens that have stopped laying eggs can still contribute to the overall functioning of your backyard flock. They can serve as companions for younger chickens, provide a sense of security within the flock, and even assist in natural pest control by foraging and scratching the ground. Older hens are often more dominant, and their presence can also contribute to the well-being and social dynamics of the flock.

Feeding hens that are no longer producing eggs can be expensive, and you may want to explore other ways to dispose of them. Depending on personal preferences and local regulations, you may choose to process non-laying hens for meat. This can be an ethical and sustainable way to utilize their resources and provide nourishment. If this is the route you wish to go down, we will discuss the intricacies of processing chickens for meat in the next chapter.

Alternatively, you might consider culling non-laying hens. If this is your preferred option, consult local authorities or agricultural extension offices to learn about appropriate methods for euthanizing and disposing of chickens.

If none of the previous options seems palatable to you, then you either need to reconcile yourself to the fact that you'll be keeping non-laying hens until they die naturally, or you can look into rehoming them. Finding someone who will take on unproductive chickens can be difficult, but city farms and animal welfare charities are good places to start.

HOW TO SELL EGGS

Selling eggs from your flock can be a rewarding endeavor, allowing you to share your fresh and delicious eggs with others. However, before embarking on this venture, it is crucial to familiarize yourself with the laws and regulations governing egg sales in your area.

As eggs are a food product, selling them is subject to specific regulations that vary by jurisdiction. It is essential to research and understand the laws applicable to your region. Check with your local authorities, such as agricultural departments or health departments, to ensure that you comply with all relevant requirements. This may include obtaining necessary permits or licenses and adhering to specific labeling and sanitation standards.

When it comes to selling your eggs, presenting them in a clean and appealing manner is essential for attracting customers. As backyard chicken keepers, we are used to eggs that are not pristine, but the general public is not! Soiled eggs should be washed in warm water and a mild detergent specifically formulated for egg cleaning. Make sure to discard any eggs that are damaged and sort the remainder based on size, color, and quality.

You will need a supply of clean and sturdy egg cartons to package your eggs. Label each carton with relevant information, including your farm name, date of packaging, and any additional information according to local regulations. Regular customers can be encouraged to return egg cartons for reuse, helping to keep costs down.

Where Can You Sell Your Eggs?

Most backyard chicken keepers start out selling surplus eggs to friends, family, coworkers, and neighbors. If you find that you still have more eggs than you can handle, a hassle-free sales route is to set up a farm stand at the entrance of your property to sell eggs directly to passing customers. These normally rely on an honesty-box payment system, so you risk losing precious eggs or hard-earned cash to unscrupulous members of the public.

Local farmers' markets can be a good option if you decide to scale your egg-selling operations up to the next level. Contact your local market organizers to inquire about vendor opportunities, regulations, and any fees or permits required. Alternatively, consider approaching local grocery stores, specialty shops, or restaurants that prioritize local and fresh produce. Community Supported Agriculture (CSA) programs, where members subscribe to receive regular deliveries of fresh produce, are also a good outlet for selling eggs.

Check out this YouTube video that demonstrates how to candle your eggs.

SUMMARY

In this chapter, we have dived into the exciting world of egg production and the art of selling your surplus egg supply. As a backyard chicken keeper, you should now be well-equipped with everything you need to know about raising a flock of productive and happy hens. So, if you dream of cracking open a delicious, golden-yolked egg laid by your own hens for breakfast every day, nothing is standing in your way!

But what if you want to explore the other aspect of chicken rearing – how difficult is it to process chickens for meat? Although it is a topic that some people might be uncomfortable with, it is a fact of life that chicken is still a popular choice on menus around the world.

So, in our final chapter, we are going to explore the ins and outs of raising chickens for meat, including how to process them and cook them to enjoy your poultry at its very best. If you're a fan of juicy, succulent chicken meat, stay tuned for the next chapter, where we'll uncover the secrets of harvesting chicken meat!

9

MEAT IS MONEY

*a*s awareness grows about the impact of food choices on our health and the environment, an increasing number of consumers are seeking sources of poultry that are not only reared with the animal's welfare in mind but also using more natural or organic methods.

The shift in consumer preference towards organic chicken meat can be attributed to two main factors. Firstly, people are increasingly conscious of the welfare issues associated with conventional chicken farming, which often involves poor conditions for the birds. Additionally, many individuals see organic meat as a safer choice for their families, as it is produced without synthetic pesticides, antibiotics, or growth hormones.

Organic farming practices are perceived to be more sustainable and environmentally friendly, minimizing the potential negative effects of conventional farming on ecosystems and water sources. Furthermore, organic meat is often associated with higher animal welfare standards, with the belief that animals raised in organic systems are treated more humanely.

Because of this, you may consider rearing chickens for meat alongside, or instead of, egg production. Whether you just want the confidence to process any surplus roosters occasionally or are planning a larger-scale operation, it is vital to be armed with the necessary information before you start.

If rearing chickens for meat is not your thing, no problem! We know plenty of chicken keepers who just have a small flock of hens for egg production and would balk at the thought of eating one of their birds.

However, the fact remains that breeding backyard chickens undoubtedly creates a surplus of roosters, and dispatching them for the table is widely regarded as a sustainable form of meat. Plus, if you've got a consistent supply of cheap chicken feed, rearing chicks is a great way to secure a source of affordable, high-quality meat for your family. So, if you're considering raising backyard chickens for meat, let's learn everything you need to know!

WHY REAR CHICKENS FOR MEAT?

It is no secret that commercial chicken farming is not a particularly high-welfare practice – those of you who enjoy spending time with your backyard flock will no doubt shudder at the sight of thousands of chickens crammed into huge barns. But aside from the improved welfare of pasture-reared chickens, there are also positive implications for human health as consumers of chicken meat.

Backyard chickens are typically raised without the use of antibiotics or hormones. They are less likely to be exposed to synthetic chemicals and pesticides commonly found in conventional feed and agricultural practices, reducing the potential for chemical residues in the meat.

Pasture-reared chickens have also been shown to have

higher nutrient content in their meat compared to conventionally raised chickens. This can bring significant health benefits to anyone who consumes chicken regularly.

Heart Health

The higher levels of omega-3 fatty acids in pasture-reared chicken can be beneficial for cardiovascular health. Omega-3 fatty acids have been shown to reduce the risk of heart disease by lowering blood pressure, reducing inflammation, and improving overall heart function. Consuming pasture-reared chicken, which naturally contains higher levels of omega-3s, can contribute to a heart-healthy diet.

Immune System Support

Pasture-reared chicken contains higher levels of vitamins A, E, and beta-carotene. These nutrients play a crucial role in supporting a healthy immune system. Vitamin A helps maintain the integrity of the skin and mucous membranes, which act as barriers against pathogens. Vitamin E is a powerful antioxidant that helps protect cells from damage, and beta-carotene is converted to vitamin A in the body and supports immune function.

Eye Health

Vitamin A and beta-carotene, both present in higher amounts in pasture-reared chicken, are essential for maintaining good vision and promoting eye health. Vitamin A plays a critical role in producing rhodopsin, a pigment necessary for low-light and color vision. Beta-carotene, a precursor to vitamin A, acts as an antioxidant and helps protect the eyes from oxidative stress.

Antioxidant Protection

The increased levels of vitamins A and E in pasture-reared chicken provide antioxidant protection to the body. Antioxidants help neutralize harmful free radicals and reduce oxidative stress, which is associated with various chronic diseases, including cancer, cardiovascular disease, and neurodegenerative disorders.

Skin Health

The combination of omega-3 fatty acids and vitamins A and E in pasture-reared chicken can benefit skin health. Omega-3s help maintain the integrity of cell membranes, promoting healthy skin structure and reducing inflammation. Vitamins A and E provide antioxidant protection, helping to combat oxidative damage and maintain the health and appearance of the skin.

Nutrient Absorption

Higher levels of nutrients in pasture-reared chickens can contribute to better overall nutrient absorption when consumed as part of a balanced diet. For example, healthy fats, such as omega-3 fatty acids, aid in absorbing fat-soluble vitamins like vitamins A and E.

THE DIFFERENCES BETWEEN REARING MEAT CHICKENS AND EGG-LAYING HENS

When it comes to raising chickens in your backyard, you'll find that there are two primary types of birds: meat chickens and egg layers. Most chicken keepers tend to keep specific breeds or types of chicken for each purpose. However, many traditional chicken breeds are good dual-purpose birds. For example, we like to have a few Brahma chickens in our flock, as they are good egg layers and very tasty, albeit slow-growing, meat birds.

Understanding the differences between rearing meat chickens and egg layers is crucial if you wish to successfully raise and process chickens for meat. To start with, meat chickens require feed that is higher in protein to support their rapid growth and muscle development. Their feed intake will need to be monitored and adjusted accordingly as they grow to maintain a healthy growth rate. It is vital to avoid overfeeding meat birds, as this can lead to health issues such as leg problems or heart strain.

Ideally, feeding meat chickens and egg-laying hens separate diets would optimize their health and nutritional needs, but it's okay to feed them the same feed if it meets the nutritional needs of both types of birds. Meat chickens may also require more living space than egg layers due to their rapid growth and larger size. They will need ample room to move around comfortably without overcrowding. Raising meat chickens in a free-range system is possible, but they may require extra protection from predators as they are not very street-smart.

Our preferred method is to keep any chickens intended for meat in a larger run and coop; the egg layers have smaller living quarters but enjoy several hours each day free-ranging across the land. The meat birds get some extra snacks and treats each day, but never more than 10% of their overall food intake. This system means that we can meet the specific nutritional requirements of all our birds while also ensuring they have adequate space and environmental enrichment to live full and happy lives.

WHEN TO PROCESS MEAT CHICKENS

Knowing when to process meat birds for the table is the key to getting deliciously tender chicken meat. In a commercial setting, fast-growing hybrids can be ready for the table in as little as six weeks, but most backyard chicken keepers opt for slower-growing birds that have fewer health problems.

Gauging the right time to process your chickens depends on the age, weight, and breed of the bird. You also need to factor in the desired meat quality, as this can change considerably over a period of just a few weeks.

Age and Weight

Most meat chickens are processed when they reach a specific age or weight range. For commercial broilers, this is usually when they are between 8 and 12 weeks of age or when they weigh around 4 to 6 pounds. However, some slower-growing heritage breeds may require a longer rearing period before reaching the desired weight.

At this age, the chicken will be near its full adult weight, but the meat will still be young and tender. Over the next few months, muscles will become toughened and sinewy through exercise, leading to tougher meat.

Growth Rate and Development

When your meat chickens are ready for processing, they should have reached a mature size, with fully developed muscle and fat deposits. Ideally, their breasts should be plump and meaty, indicating optimal meat quality.

Breed Recommendations

Different meat chicken breeds may have specific recommendations for processing. If you sourced your birds from a breeder or hatchery, they should provide you with guidance on when to process them for the best meat quality.

Personal Preference

The joy of rearing chickens for meat is that you get to pick the exact time to process them to get the flavor of meat you prefer! Younger chickens have more tender meat, whereas older birds have a fuller, richer flavor.

HOW TO DISPATCH A MEAT CHICKEN

When it comes to dispatching a chicken, it's essential to prioritize humane and swift methods to minimize stress and pain for the bird. If you have never done this before, it is a good idea to ask a more experienced chicken keeper to assist you.

Before dispatching a chicken, choose the location carefully and prepare the area and equipment. The whole operation needs to be calm and swift to avoid undue stress to the bird. Bear in mind that any remaining birds will hear and smell what is going on, so keep the processing area as far away from your chicken coop as possible.

To dispatch a meat chicken, you will need a sharp knife or poultry shears, a killing cone or a secure surface, a bucket or container for blood collection, and access to a clean water source. At this point, it is also a good idea to ensure you have everything ready to harvest the chicken meat once the bird is dead.

The two most common methods used to dispatch a chicken are cervical dislocation (also known as neck dislocation) and throat cutting. Choose the method you are most comfortable with, and that aligns with your skills and local regulations.

Whichever method you use, minimizing how much the bird can move is crucial. To do this, secure the chicken in a killing cone or hold it firmly against a secure surface. This will prevent the bird from flapping its wings and potentially causing injury.

Cervical dislocation involves manually dislocating the chicken's neck, causing immediate spinal cord damage and loss of consciousness. Grasp the chicken's head firmly with one hand while holding the body steady with the other hand. With a quick, firm motion, twist or pull the head upwards and away from the body to dislocate the neck. This method requires skill and precision to be done correctly.

With the throat-cutting method, the major blood vessels in the chicken's neck are severed, resulting in rapid blood loss and loss of consciousness. Locate the major blood vessels in the chicken's neck by feeling the soft spot just below the jawline. Using a sharp knife or poultry shears, make a deep, quick cut across the neck, severing both the carotid arteries and the jugular veins. It is important to make a quick, deep cut to ensure a swift and humane process.

After dispatching the chicken, allow it to bleed out fully by hanging it over a bucket or container to collect the blood. You can use the collected blood for composting or dispose of it according to local regulations.

HOW TO HARVEST CHICKEN MEAT

Once your chicken has been dispatched, it is time to turn your attention to harvesting the chicken meat. It is important to note that the methods described here are for informational purposes only – we highly recommend that you seek out a training course in your local area, as there is no substitute for practical, hands-on experience when it comes to harvesting chicken meat. Additionally, it is crucial to ensure that any harvesting methods align with local regulations and guidelines.

Before beginning the chicken harvesting process, you need to gather the necessary supplies. Here are some commonly used tools:

- De-boning Knife: A sharp, de-boning knife is required to accurately remove the chicken meat.

- Lung Puller: A lung puller is used to, you guessed it, remove the lungs from the chicken's chest cavity.

- Large Pot: Your pot needs to be large enough to fit your chicken when you scald it with hot water. Scalding the chicken in hot water helps loosen the feathers for easier plucking.

- Cooler: A cooler filled with ice or cold water is used to cool and store the processed chickens.

Once the chicken has been hung until all the blood has drained out, it is briefly immersed in hot water to loosen the feathers. This process, known as scalding, makes feather removal easier. The feathers can then be carefully plucked without causing damage to the skin.

The chicken is now ready for gutting and trimming. The chicken's body cavity is carefully opened, and the internal organs, including the crop, intestines, and lungs, are removed. The body is rinsed thoroughly to remove any remaining debris, and the skin is inspected for any remaining feathers or debris and cleaned as necessary.

Suppose you are leaving your chicken whole for roasting. In that case, you may choose to carry out additional processing, such as removing the feet and head. The chicken legs can then be trussed up, ready for cooking.

Or, break down the chicken into portions if you aren't planning to cook it all at once. There are various techniques available depending on your preferences. You can opt to remove and separate the breasts, thighs, wings, or drumsticks. Another option is to quarter or spatchcock the chicken before preparing it for the pot.

PREPARING CHICKEN FOR CULINARY PERFECTION

If you attempted to cook your home-reared chicken in the same way as a pack of commercially-reared poultry from the store, you might be sorely disappointed! It is a sad fact that we've become accustomed to mass-produced, poor-quality chicken meat, and many people have forgotten what 'real' chicken tastes like. However, with this fantastic flavor comes the risk of tough, sinewy meat that is often considered unpalatable.

However, by understanding the steps involved in preparing home-reared chicken for culinary purposes, you'll be able to create delicious chicken dishes that showcase the flavors and textures of your carefully-nurtured poultry.

Before we talk about the best way to cook home-reared chicken meat, let's talk about why it is so different from mass-produced poultry. Your carefully nurtured meat chickens have most likely had a very different life from a commercially-raised bird, with more opportunities for foraging and roaming, a more varied diet, and a longer lifespan.

While all of these things are beneficial to the chicken's

health and well-being, they ultimately alter the meat's taste and texture. Fast-growing commercially-reared broilers are fed intensively on a high-protein diet and have little opportunity to roam, so the meat tends to be a more tender texture due to a lack of muscle development. Many people describe this meat as soft and watery – not something we would consider to be desirable properties on our dinner plates!

In contrast, pasture-reared chickens have a fuller, richer flavor and a more robust texture due to their varied diet and increased activity levels. Some people claim that the meat has a grassy flavor, while others say it tastes like chicken used to when they were young.

However, these differences in flavor and texture can be quite pronounced, particularly in older roosters. In this situation, the meat is often described as gamey, and the sinewy texture can be tough and unpleasant. This is because of increased muscle development in older, larger birds, and you will need to alter your cooking style to account for this.

So, how do you cook a pasture-reared chicken? Well, one that has been processed at exactly the right age can be roasted just like a commercially-reared chicken, but you may find that cooking times are shorter. This is because the water content of the meat will be lower, so it reaches the optimum cooking temperature faster.

For an older bird that is more likely to have tough, sinewy meat, you will need to alter your cooking techniques to account for this. The first thing to remember is that the meat will need aging – leave the bird in the refrigerator for at least four days before cooking it. This allows the muscle fibers to relax and tenderize, reducing the risk of tough, unpalatable meat.

We find the best results for cooking an older chicken come from using low, slow cooking methods with plenty of moisture – a slow-cooker is the ideal way to do these birds justice. Marinating or brining the meat beforehand can also help to add flavor and moisture to the meat.

Our favorite way to cook an older rooster or hen to make the most of their delicious meat is to marinate the meat in brine or buttermilk for 24 hours beforehand. The carcass is then cut into quarters and slow-cooked in a mix of herbs, garlic, onion, celery, and white wine, making sure it is fully submerged in the liquid. After several hours over low heat, the meat will be incredibly succulent, and so tender that it just falls off the bone. With great flavor comes great responsibility.

HOW TO SELL CHICKEN MEAT

Scaling up your meat chicken production level to the point where you can sell chicken meat is a big leap – processing a few birds to share with the family is one thing, but a commercial venture is quite another. Whether you're a local farmer, a small-scale producer, or an entrepreneur in the poultry business, understanding the regulations and food safety practices, finding customers, and effectively communicating with them are all crucial aspects of successfully selling chicken meat.

Before venturing into selling chicken meat, it is essential to familiarize yourself with the regulations and guidelines set by local and national authorities. Ensure that you comply with licensing, labeling, and packaging requirements, as well as any specific poultry processing and distribution regulations. Your local authority may run training courses for aspiring meat sellers, and your premises will likely need to be inspected to ensure they are up to standard.

Maintaining high food safety standards is paramount when selling chicken meat. Adhere to best practices for handling, storing, and processing poultry products. Implement proper hygiene protocols, temperature controls, and packaging practices to ensure the safety and quality of your product.

Selling fresh chicken meat can pose challenges in maintaining a consistent supply to meet customer demand. On the other hand, frozen chicken offers advantages in managing stock levels, making it a viable choice for small-scale producers or farmers seeking to sell their chicken meat directly to consumers.

Before embarking on a chicken-selling business venture, it is important to identify your target market and develop strategies to reach them. Explore local farmers' markets, community events, or establish relationships with local retailers or restaurants that prioritize locally sourced products. Make use of online platforms, social media, or even create your own website to spread the word about your chicken meat and connect with potential customers.

As a chicken meat retailer, it's important to effectively market the quality standards of your product. Realistically, your meat will have a higher price than store-bought chicken, it's crucial to highlight the unique qualities that make it stand out. Be transparent about organic farming practices, higher animal welfare, and sustainability, as these aspects can appeal to consumers looking for ethically produced chicken meat.

One of the aspects that can put many people off rearing chickens for meat is the time spent processing them. If you don't have the facilities or expertise to process large amounts of chicken meat on your own, consider partnering with a local poultry processor. This will obviously reduce your profit margin but means you can spend more time focussing on rearing poultry rather than processing the meat.

If you choose to go down this route, research and establish relationships with reputable processors that align with your values and high-quality standards. Effective communication with your processor is essential to ensure that your chicken meat is processed according to your specifications. Clearly discuss your requirements, including cuts, packaging, labeling, and additional processing steps.

As we discussed previously, you are unlikely to be able to compete with commercial chicken farms when it comes to pricing your meat. Rearing pasture-raised meat chickens is more costly because the chickens live longer lives. Still, for many consumers, the benefits outweigh this extra cost. Set appropriate pricing for your chicken meat based on factors such as production costs, market demand, and the quality of your product. Consider the value that customers place on organic, local, or pasture-raised options and adjust your pricing accordingly.

SUMMARY

Although raising chickens for meat is not something that every backyard chicken keeper will be keen to embark on, it is an aspect of chicken keeping that more and more people are beginning to explore. By rearing your own chickens for meat, you can guarantee a supply of healthy, delicious food for your family that comes from birds that have lived happy and fulfilled lives.

Whether you just wish to process a surplus rooster or two on an occasional basis or are embarking on a commercial chicken meat venture by producing organic, local, and cage-free poultry, you are fostering sustainable farming practices, promoting animal welfare, and nourishing your family with healthier options.

Now, as we conclude our journey, it is crucial to

remember the positive impact your choices can have on the world. Take pride in what you have learned by reading this book and the choices you are making. You have the power to create change, one chicken at a time!

As you move forward, we hope that you will share your newfound knowledge and experiences with others, encouraging them to join you on this path toward a better future. By taking the time to learn about raising healthy and happy chickens, you have shown dedication and a commitment to making informed choices. Embrace the lessons you have learned and let them guide you as you continue to nurture a healthier and more compassionate world.

AFTERWORD

Congratulations! You have reached the end of our chicken journey, equipped with valuable knowledge and insights into all the aspects of raising backyard chickens. By engaging with the chapters of this book, you have gained a deeper understanding of chickens, their well-being, and the choices we can make to improve their lives and our own.

Throughout this book, we have aimed to equip you with the knowledge and confidence to embark on your own chicken-raising journey. We have thoroughly explored the ins and outs of raising backyard chickens, from choosing suitable breeds to providing proper nutrition and creating a safe and comfortable environment for your flock. By learning about these essential topics, you should have a newfound confidence in your understanding of the key aspects of backyard chicken care.

With the right knowledge and dedication, we firmly believe that anyone can raise backyard chickens and enjoy all the benefits they bring. By implementing the strategies outlined in each chapter of our book, you can create a thriving and happy flock that provides you with fresh eggs, natural pest control, and a deep connection to nature.

Don't forget that we all have to start somewhere – we were once novice chicken keepers ourselves, and we had all the same questions and doubts that any new chicken owner has. Only through years of experience and learning have we gained the knowledge we shared with you within this book. By applying the principles shared in this guide, we have witnessed our flock flourish and enjoy an abundance of eggs, a healthier garden, and a greater appreciation for sustainable living. Now, armed with the knowledge gained from this book, you too can embark on your own chicken-raising adventure.

We would like to extend our sincere thanks to all the readers who have joined us on this educational journey. We hope that our book has been an invaluable resource, empowering you to embark on a fulfilling and sustainable backyard chicken-raising experience. If you have found this book useful, we would appreciate it if you could spread the word amongst any aspiring chicken keepers by leaving a review.

"Good luck on your journey, and may your new flock bring you joy, self-sufficiency, and a deep sense of satisfaction. Remember, the joys of raising chickens extend far beyond their eggs; they become cherished members of your family and bring a sense of connection to the natural world. Now, it's time to take action, enjoy the rewards, and continue learning as you embark on this extraordinary adventure. There really is no better time to embrace this opportunity and create a thriving haven for your feathered friends. Happy chicken raising!"

— TYLER AND LEANN BRISTOL

Inspire a New Chicken Owner!

Once you have your flock, you'll never look back – you're about to embark on one of the most rewarding ventures of your life... and that makes you the perfect person to inspire someone else.

Simply by sharing your honest opinion of this book, you'll show new readers where they can find all the guidance they need to start raising their own chickens.

Thank you so much for your support. We wish you every success with your new flock.

Review link:

REFERENCES

Cooped Up Life. (n.d.). Chicken Statistics. https://coopeduplife.com/chicken-statistics/

Backyard Chicken Project. (n.d.). Chicken Facts. https://backyardchicken project.com/chicken-facts/

Backyard Poultry. (n.d.). Can I Raise Chickens in My Area? https://backyard poultry.iamcountryside.com/chickens-101/can-i-raise-chickens-in-my-area/

Backyard Poultry. (n.d.). How Many Chickens Do I Need? https://backyard poultry.iamcountryside.com/chickens-101/how-many-chickens-do-i-need/

Backyard Poultry. (n.d.). Raising Backyard Chickens: The Basics of Feeding and Watering. https://backyardpoultry.iamcountryside.com/feed-health/raising-backyard-chickens-the-basics-of-feeding-and-watering/

Backyard Chicken Project. (n.d.). 6 Questions to Ask Yourself Before Getting Chickens. https://backyardchickenproject.com/6-questions-to-ask-your self-before-getting-chickens/

Countryside Network. (n.d.). 12 Vital Questions to Ask Before Getting Chickens. https://countrysidenetwork.com/daily/poultry/chickens-101/getting-started-chickens-12-vital-questions/

Farm and Dairy. (n.d.). 9 Basic Considerations for Backyard Poultry. https://www.farmanddairy.com/top-stories/9-basic-considerations-for-back yard-poultry/478093.html

Fresh Eggs Daily. (n.d.). 10 Things to Consider Before You Start. https://www.fresheggsdaily.blog/2018/04/10-things-to-consider-before-you-start.html

Fresh Eggs Daily. (n.d.). 10 Things You Should Know About Raising Chick-ens. https://www.fresheggsdaily.blog/2014/04/10-things-you-should-know-about-raising.html

Happy Chicken Coop. (n.d.). The Complete Guide to Chicken Feed. https://www.thehappychickencoop.com/the-complete-guide-to-chicken-feed/

Heritage Acres Market. (n.d.). Backyard Chicken Survey. https://www.heritageacresmarket.com/backyard-chicken-survey/

Jabr, F. (2017, December 11). Fowl language: AI decodes the nuances of chicken "Speech". Scientific American. https://www.scientificamerican.com/article/fowl-language-ai-decodes-the-nuances-of-chicken-ldquo-speech-rdquo/"

Khan, R. U., Naz, S., De Marzo, D., Dimuccio, M. M., Bozzo, G., Tufarelli, V.,

Losacco, C., & Ragni, M. (2022). Aloe vera: A sustainable green alternative to exclude antibiotics in modern poultry production. Antibiotics (Basel), 12(1), 44. https://doi.org/10.3390/antibiotics12010044

KH Pet. (n.d.). How Much Space Do Chickens Need? https://khpet.com/blogs/farm/how-much-space-do-chickens-need

Morning Chores. (n.d.). Choosing a Chicken Breed - Beginner's Guide. https://morningchores.com/choosing-a-chicken-breed/

My Pet Chicken. (n.d.). Chickens: The Perfect Beginner's Livestock. https://www.mypetchicken.com/backyard-chickens/chicken-help/Chickens-The-Perfect-Beginners-Livestock-H166.aspx

My Pet Chicken. (n.d.). What Do Chickens Eat? https://www.mypetchicken.com/backyard-chickens/chicken-help/What-Do-Chickens-Eat-H1.aspx

Ohio State University. (n.d.). ANR-60: Selecting Chicken Breeds for Small and Backyard Flocks. https://ohioline.osu.edu/factsheet/anr-60

Pete and Gerry's Organics. (n.d.). Local Laws for Raising Backyard Chickens. https://www.peteandgerrys.com/blog/local-laws-for-raising-backyard-chickens

Poultry Extension. (n.d.). Space Allowances in Housing for Small and Backyard Poultry Flocks. https://poultry.extension.org/articles/getting-started-with-small-and-backyard-poultry/housing-for-small-and-backyard-poultry-flocks/space-allowances-in-housing-for-small-and-backyard-poultry-flocks/

Purina Mills. (n.d.). Can I Raise Backyard Chickens in My Area? https://www.purinamills.com/chicken-feed/education/detail/can-i-raise-backyard-chickens-in-my-area

Rodale's Organic Life. (n.d.). 10 Essential Tips for Raising Chickens. https://www.rodalesorganiclife.com/garden/10-essential-tips-for-raising-chickens

Sunset. (n.d.). 6 Questions to Ask Yourself Before Getting Chickens. https://www.sunset.com/garden/how-to-raise-backyard-chickens

The Happy Chicken Coop. (n.d.). Do You Need a Rooster? https://www.thehappychickencoop.com/do-you-need-a-rooster/

The Happy Chicken Coop. (n.d.). How Many Chickens Should I Get? https://www.thehappychickencoop.com/how-many-chickens-should-i-get/

The Happy Chicken Coop. (n.d.). How Many Roosters Should You Have? https://www.thehappychickencoop.com/how-many-roosters-should-you-have/

The Happy Chicken Coop. (n.d.). How Much Room Do Chickens Need? https://www.thehappychickencoop.com/how-much-room-do-chickens-need/

The Happy Chicken Coop. (n.d.). The Pros and Cons of Keeping Roosters.

https://www.thehappychickencoop.com/the-pros-and-cons-of-keeping-roosters/

The Old Farmer's Almanac. (n.d.). Raising Chickens 101: Choosing Chicken Breeds. https://www.almanac.com/raising-chickens-101-choosing-chicken-breeds

The Poultry Site. (n.d.). Keeping Roosters in Backyard Flocks. https://thepoultrysite.com/articles/keeping-roosters-in-backyard-flocks

The Spruce Eats. (n.d.). Can You Eat a Fertilized Egg? https://www.thespruceeats.com/can-you-eat-a-fertilized-egg-4684124

The Spruce Eats. (n.d.). How to Humanely Euthanize a Chicken. https://www.thespruceeats.com/humanely-euthanize-a-chicken-4688112

The Spruce Pets. (n.d.). Feeding Chickens: What You Need to Know. https://www.thesprucepets.com/feeding-chickens-551798

The Spruce Pets. (n.d.). How to Clean and Store Fresh Eggs. https://www.thesprucepets.com/how-to-clean-and-store-fresh-eggs-3016706

The Spruce Pets. (n.d.). Should You Raise Chickens? https://www.thesprucepets.com/should-you-raise-chickens-4580453

The Way Homestead. (n.d.). How Many Chickens Should You Get? https://thewayhomestead.com/how-many-chickens-should-you-get/

University of Kentucky Cooperative Extension Service. (n.d.). Proper Handling and Care of Fresh Eggs. https://extension.ca.uky.edu/files/efpdfs/ef606.pdf

University of Maine Cooperative Extension. (n.d.). Watering Backyard Poultry. https://extension.umaine.edu/publications/2025e/

35 quotes about communication for inspiring team collaboration. (2022, May 5). Smart Board for Remote Work | Vibe. https://vibe.us/blog/35-quotes-about-communication/